BOILING POINT

52 RECIPES + COLUMNS BY PROLIFIC COLUMNIST JIM HILLIBISH

Boiling Point

52 RECIPES + COLUMNS BY PROLIFIC COLUMNIST JIM HILLIBISH

Printed and bound in the United States of America.

ISBN: 978-0-9988981-0-0

10 9 8 7 6 5 4 3 2 1

THE CANTON REPOSITORY
CantonRep.com

THE CANTON REPOSITORY | GATEHOUSE OHIO MEDIA
500 MARKET AVENUE S, CANTON, OHIO 44702
(330) 580-8300 | CANTONREP.COM

JIM PORTER, PUBLISHER & CEO
JESS BENNETT, VICE PRESIDENT, MAGAZINE DIVISION
RICH DESROSIERS, EXECUTIVE EDITOR
LAURA KESSEL, ENGAGEMENT EDITOR
KELSEY REINHART, MAGAZINE DIVISION EDITOR
GARY BROWN, EDITOR-AT-LARGE
MURPHY REDMOND, COVER AND BOOK DESIGN
MICHAEL WEISS, COVER ILLUSTRATION

COLUMNS & RECIPES COMPILED BY GARY BROWN AND
KATHLEEN HILLIBISH FROM FAMILY COLLECTION OF JIM'S WORK

JIM HILLIBISH'S KITCHEN IN WINTER ALWAYS WAS WARM—TOASTY ENOUGH TO DRIVE AWAY THE HARSHNESS OF WINTER.

Comfort was a watchword for Bish in these coldest of months. And, so, he turned up the heat, and not just with the thermostat. Spices did the trick for some food—chili comes to mind. But for a multitude of other dishes, it was merely a warmth derived from the care taken in the preparation of the meals and the pleasant companionship that could be expected from sharing the results of his recipes.

_____

A FRESHNESS WAS IN THE AIR EACH SPRING, AND THERE ANNUALLY WAS A BRIGHTNESS IN JIM HILLIBISH'S FOOD FEATURES, AS WELL.

Oh, the familiar traditional food still was remembered in his writing. But, about this time of year, Bish's mind seemed to be moving on to fresh dishes or new cooking methods to make meals taste fresh, even if they were made from frozen ingredients. Jim's world of food came alive in the spring.

When Mother Nature turned up the heat, Jim Hillibish found a way for food to help us chill out.

Still, Jim wasn't against lighting a fire under us—well, beside us—for summer grilling. And he was known to load up a picnic basket with summer treats, or spread them out on a backyard patio table. Summer was a season to celebrate, Jim believed. Sometimes you did that with tomatoes, and other times it was with ears of sweet corn. And who knew that the way to a woman's heart was as simple as making a gazpacho salad?

Autumn was a time to dwell on seasonal foods, and Jim Hillibish served up an abundance of appropriate recipes.

They included foods suitable for cooling autumn days and surprisingly warm days that seemed to return to summer. Personal favorites are homegrown peach cobbler and homemade sorbet ... but we may be dwelling less on the desserts and more on Jim bringing it all home.

Summer

Autumn

Holidays

Turkey. Jim Hillibish's columns around the holidays frequently talked turkey.

Turkey meals. Turkey leftovers. Turkey Bowls. Thanksgiving, Christmas and New Year's Eve and Day were so much on the minds of Repository readers each year that Jim wouldn't dare let them pass without sharing with those who followed his food writing. Devoted readers likely would have been disappointed if he hadn't helped them prepare some holiday treat. A few cookies. An appetizer. Some side dish. The advice always was tailored to suit the changing times in which the holidays were celebrated. And, his words looked back to holidays that the writer remembered, and traditions that guided his family gatherings.

—GARY BROWN

JIM HILLIBISH,

a graduate of Glenwood High School and Kent State University, worked in the newsroom of The Canton Repository for 44 years—a career briefly interrupted when he served in the U.S. Army early in the 1970s.

He covered every major beat at the newspaper and was both city editor and lifestyle editor, as well as chief of the newspaper's North Bureau, then later created the newspaper's website and served for years as its webmaster. Varied in his interests, he also wrote weekly human interest columns and penned gardening and computer columns. But, it was his love of food that perhaps captured readers' interest in greatest numbers.

His weekly "Boiling Point" column in The Repository's food pages was devoured with enthusiasm, and the recipes he provided readers in those essays—many of the recipes for foods that he and his wife Kathleen Fernandez Hillibish prepared in their kitchen—were part of his lasting legacy when he died in 2014 of renal cancer.

In 2017, the Plain Local Schools Foundation & Alumni Association honored Jim in its Hall of Distinction.

Why Bish Loved to Cook

If Jim Hillibish and Paul Simon wrote a song together, the title might have been "50 Ways To Love Your Cooking."

This "Boiling Point" column, published on August 4, 2004, was Jim's list of his "50 joys of cooking." It might help bring a better understanding of Bish and the common way he approached cooking, to peruse it again.

The more you cook, the more you like:

1 Picnic potlucks
2 Guests who wash dishes
3 Friends who bring blueberries
4 Charcoal grills
5 Caramelizing
6 Non-picky children
7 "Gimme a little more of that."
8 Grandma's iron skillets
9 Wine, inside the pot and you
10 Aromas
11 Saimi and Jenny (Bergmann and Mastroianni, fellow food writers and friends)
12 Vegetable gardens
13 Herbs in morning dew
14 FoodTV
15 Bacon wraps
16 Corn so fresh it squeaks
17 Farmers' markets
18 Help
19 Gizmos
20 Mom's old recipe box
21 Oven cleaner
22 Freezer space
23 Balsamic vinegar
24 Cilantro
25 Homemade ravioli
26 Your Italian neighbors
27 Harvest trading
28 Garlic breath
29 Onion fingers
30 Gourmet sections
31 Coffee conversations
32 Two hours for dinner
33 "Let's eat."
34 12-place settings
35 Freshly ground pepper
36 Nutmeg graters
37 Sharing recipes
38 Epicurious.com
39 Freshly squeezed lemon juice
40 Capers on salmon
41 Pesto
42 Marinades
43 Smoker grills
44 Homemade pasta parties
45 "Kiss the cook" aprons
46 Pizza delivery
47 Nonstick bread pans
48 Coupons
49 Stone-ground mustard
50 Other folks' cooking

Remembering Jim's recipes is like sharing his kitchen

Few among us got the chance to cook with Jim Hillibish, though most of us who read his food writing likely felt like we did.

As each week's Boiling Point column or food feature was published by one of The Canton Repository's most popular food writers, many readers no doubt came away from devouring his words with the full and satisfied feeling that they just shared time with him in his kitchen. Surely they thought they knew him well enough to be a guest in his home.

Part of the reason for that closeness was his style. Jim was a storyteller. Rarely did Bish's culinary words get printed without a story being included in them at some point in the column. Personal experience. Food history. Dinner memories. Trendy culinary news. Gardening details, which is how the food got to his and our kitchens in the first place.

Bish didn't so much write about food as he lived it. Certainly he brought the food knowledge he served up to life with words written in his unique style.

Later in life, Jim didn't travel much, but he still was able to recapture moments from previous trips and widen our breadth of knowledge of the geographical nature of the culinary arts. In those columns, he would regale readers with his conversations with locals well met. He would remind us all that our food wasn't the only food, and our culinary world was enlarged because of his recognition of the diversity of food culture.

Both ethnic and family food traditions drive our dining habits, Jim knew. And as his family got smaller—as members of all our families were lost—Jim was able to keep alive meaningful food traditions from memory. His memories. The recollections of others.

Our world was quickening, of course. As our lives became more complicated, Jim was able to "keep it simple," as he liked to say about his cooking. No one went back to basics better than Bish—before succumbing to his nearly constant state of curiosity and suggesting little changes to what was comfortable in order to improve upon the result.

When technology began to change our kitchen techniques, Bish, both a traditionalist and a "techie" at heart, didn't rebel against the modern methods. He embraced them, at least long enough to try them, discovering which new devices were convenient to his cooking and which new products were no more than passing fads—distracting at best and destructive to the quality of food at their worst.

Still, far more important to Jim than the tools of his cooking trade were the people who made use of them—the men and women who shared their food successes and failures with Jim on a nearly daily basis. Jim gave credit to them because credit was due. Friends, family, co-workers, newly acquainted strangers and longtime readers all found their way into his columns. That's why you'll find in this volume such recipes as "Mom's Biscuits," "Milly Carper's Rhubarb Custard Pie," "Mary Coletti's Pizzelles" and "Pam McGowen's Best Potato Salad You Ever Ate."

Oh, and "Jim's Garlic Mashed Potatoes" are in here, too. This is, after all, a book about Bish and some of his favorite recipes.

Jim didn't name the smashed spuds after himself, of course. An editor did.

If you knew him—and it seemed sometimes as though everyone did—you know that for Jim it wasn't so much about the cook as it was about the food. For Bish, his love always was for the food—and for those who loved to read about it. So, in a sense, this isn't just Jim Hillibish's book. It's your book, too. Enjoy.

SEEKING COMFORT FROM THE COLD

Dare we call it SOUPER BOWL?

SOUP SOLVES THE MAJOR QUANDARY OF SUPER BOWL PARTY SUNDAY.

You need a light meal built a day ahead to permit you to watch the ads, or perhaps the game if you're really into it.

Then again, perhaps you're primed for a steamy bowl of thick chili or cheesy-spicy quesadillas or a brace of enchiladas or simply a lush bean dip with salsa on your appetizer buffet.

Imagine handling all this with one recipe.

That's our five-way white chili, winner of the 18th Street Grand Award Souper Bowl Championship.

It started with thoughts of your usual red chili with beef, but that seemed so prosaic. I wanted something unique and Tex-Mex, and remembered a white chili soup I enjoyed on a mountain-climbing trip in the Rockies. I found it on a street-corner lunch cart in Aspen, Colorado, brewed by a retired New York City firefighter.

It took a Saturday morning to reconstruct, and then things started getting weird. My white chili soup began suggesting other dishes. I settled on the chili, quesadillas and bean dip—all from one recipe.

It blew the crowd away, something authentically Tex-Mex with deeply melded flavors. These are dishes that adjust well to spicy preferences, so serve with a variety of hot sauces and the all-important green salsa. By popular acclaim, I'm back up to the plate again this season.

Enough, here are the recipes.

BOILING POINT, JAN. 23, 2013 • Jim loved to entertain and offered advice for appetizers and entrées for almost every national party occasion through the years. Food for football's Super Bowl was one of his most consistent topics.

1 1/2 POUNDS GROUND CHICKEN

1 MEDIUM RED ONION, CHOPPED

1 TEASPOON OLIVE OIL

1 MEDIUM BELL PEPPER, RED, CHOPPED

1 MEDIUM GREEN PEPPER, POBLANO, CHOPPED

1 CUP CELERY, FINELY CHOPPED

2 14-OUNCE CANS WHITE NORTHERN BEANS

2 TO 3 CUPS CHICKEN BROTH, OR MORE

1 TEASPOON BROWN SUGAR

1 TEASPOON OREGANO, FLAKES

1 TEASPOON CHILI POWDER

1/4 TEASPOON RED PEPPER FLAKES

1/4 TEASPOON CAYENNE PEPPER

4 TO 5 CLOVES GARLIC, MINCED

HOT PEPPER SAUCE TO TASTE

1 CUP GRATED, WHITE CHEESE
SUCH AS MONTEREY JACK

1 CUP FRESH CILANTRO OR PARSLEY,
DICED, FOR GARNISH

4 SLICES BACON, FRIED, DRAINED
AND CHOPPED, OPTIONAL GARNISH

DISH NO. 1: TEX-MEX WHITE BEAN SOUP

Brown chicken in oil with onions in a chili pot. Drain and add remaining ingredients except for cheese and garnish. Bring to a boil. Reduce heat and cover. Simmer for two hours. Serve with cheese and cilantro on the side, also a stack of flour tortillas browned in olive oil and quartered, served warm.

Notes: Some like it thick, some thin. Use chicken stock to adjust it. You must make this a day ahead and refrigerate overnight to allow the flavors to meld.

Serves 8 in medium soup bowls with melted cheese on top. Run under the broiler at the last minute. Pickled jalapeño rings are nice on the side.

DISH NO. 2: WHITE CHILI

Cut the soup stock in half. Add one 14-ounce can of kidney beans, drained, one can of chopped sweet jalapeño peppers and one can of hot, with juice. Adjust thickness to your taste with more chicken broth if needed. Adjust spiciness with pepper sauce.

DISH NO. 3: BEAN DIP

Cook down 3 cups chili until thickened or use a flour and water mixture. In a blender, puree until smooth. Add other half, chill and serve with warmed taco chips or flour tortilla triangles.

DISH NO. 4: QUESADILLAS

Warm 6 medium flour tortillas. Spread each with cream cheese, then a layer of bean dip. Top with jack cheese and another tortilla. Fry each in olive oil until brown. Let sit for 5 minutes and then cut into quarters pizza style and serve with a side of green or red salsa, chopped scallions with stems and corn relish.

DISH NO. 5: ENCHILADAS

Make chili but use chopped, cooked chicken instead of ground. Spoon lengthwise across medium-size soft-flour tortillas. Roll up and place in a flat, greased baking dish. Spoon more chili over enchiladas, cover and bake for 30 minutes at 350 degrees. Spread cheese on top and finish baking uncovered, about 15 minutes. Serve beside finely shredded lettuce salad with salsa and a dollop of sour cream or guacamole.

WHATEVER CITY CHICKEN IS THIS YEAR...
IT'S NOT CHICKEN

So WHAT WILL THE CITY CHICKEN OF THE 2000s BE MADE OF? CHOPPED LIVER?

Perhaps, if it's cheap.

After opening my gas bill, I figured it's time to start rolling out the Depression-era dishes. That means city chicken.

The odyssey of this comfort food started early in the 1900s and mirrors our nation's hard times. Chicken then was costly, if you could find it. This was before the era of poultry factories. You raised your own or knew a farmer.

Veal was cheap and plentiful. So, someone crafted a skewered recipe (in more than one way) that looked like a chicken drumstick but was made of breaded veal.

Folks pretended it was chicken. Soon, it managed to gain a reputation for itself, and the "chicken" part remained in the name only (along with a strange dash of poultry seasoning).

A few decades later, veal was skyrocketing. The only cheap meat was nasty old stew beef. City chicken easily made the jump.

Later, beef hit the roof, but pork was cheap. You know what happened to city chicken.

Somewhere along the way, real chicken got cheap, and city chicken assimilated that, too, coming full circle. Maybe they called it "city chicken chicken."

These days, some cooks use all three—beef, pork and chicken—for city chicken. They want all their recipe bases covered.

Anyway, your city chicken depends on when and where you were born, and that makes the recipe interesting because there's more than one. I started an email battle with a friend by asking for her city chicken recipe. That touched off a 60-day war of words over exactly what is city chicken. It's whatever you've got in the meat keeper.

Consider this: City chicken in our stores is all pork. In stores in Pennsylvania, it's pork and veal. In the South, they "chicken fry" pork and beef in a similar manner but without the skewers. Hello?

The only thing that every city chicken recipe shares is slow cooking that tenderizes the cheapest of meat. That's why it endures.

Another important ingredient: wooden skewers. It doesn't cook right without them, and all meat packages labeled "city chicken" have them. Meat on a stick bakes packed together, and this tenderizes it.

We wash and save our skewers because we're frugal. That way we can make city chicken out of anything handy.

The recipes all call for breading, and there's a right way to it. Cube the meat and dust it with cornstarch in a plastic bag. Then tightly skewer about five pieces on a stick. Then dip it into stirred egg. Then roll it in the bread of cracker crumbs, your choice. Some use crushed corn flakes. You might add some fresh chopped rosemary to the crumbs.

Then lightly brown the skewers on all sides in vegetable shortening. Finally, bake them at 350 degrees covered for 30 minutes (to steam them). City chicken should be flavorful, tender and not dried out.

You'll find some thin drippings in the bottom of the dish, and they'll make a nice gravy. Thicken with a little flour. Bake potatoes alongside to save on energy.

Here's the basic recipe, diplomatically adjusted. Refrigerating the meat with the milk is an old tenderizing trick. If you're combining meats, alternate them on the skewer.

Resist the temptation to place onion and pepper slicers between the chunks of meat. These are shish kabobs and a different story.

BOILING POINT, JAN. 17, 2001 • While Jim was well aware that good food was born from the best ingredients, he had a thrifty side to him, as well. And some of his ways for cutting the costs of the family food budget had a firm foundation in our history.

1 POUND MEAT CHUNKS
(PORK, VEAL, BEEF OR CHICKEN, OR A COMBINATION)

1/2 CUP MILK

1/3 CUP CORNSTARCH

1 TEASPOON PAPRIKA

1/2 TEASPOON POULTRY SEASONING

1 CUP FINE BREAD CRUMBS OR CRACKER MEAL

2 LARGE EGGS, STIRRED

1/3 CUP VEGETABLE SHORTENING

1 CUP MEAT BROTH

6 WOODEN SKEWERS

SALT AND FRESHLY GROUND PEPPER

Cut meat into chunks and refrigerate for at least two hours in the milk, paprika and poultry seasoning.

Dust meat chunks in a bag of cornstarch. Skewer tightly, 5 pieces per stick. Roll skewers in egg and then in crumbs.

Heat oven to 350 degrees. Lightly brown skewers on all sides in shortening in a skillet for a few minutes. Drain on paper towels and place in baking dish. Add broth. Cover and bake 30 minutes. Add more broth if necessary. Then uncover and bake another 30 minutes.

Thicken remaining liquid with flour to make gravy. Season and serve. Serves 4.

The cooked skewers freeze well, ready for that modern convenience, the microwave.

BAKING BREAD

GO AHEAD, TRY IT— YOU **WILL** LIKE IT

BREAD BAKERS REMAIN A HEARTY AND HARDY LOT.

Pangs of self-doubt arise as we stare blankly at the neatly stacked loaves in the market. It takes but a minute to buy one, an afternoon to make one.

"Bird feed," we mutter as we pass, promising to hit the mixing bowl. Besides, there's no football on.

I could sit here and pound my typewriter all day about the joy of baked-from-scratch bread and still miss the point. The point is that when you slice into one of those golden loaves and ladle on the butter and jam, well, no words approach being there.

I can hear the "Oh, yeah?" chorus from here. Bread making seems a tedious mystery, a time consumer from the ancient era of one bread-winner at work and one bread maker at home. Besides, why go to all the bother for an item that wraps around lunch meat?

Fools, these, for there is no excuse, technical or aesthetic, not to try at least a few loaves. Then, we gotcha.

I've heard many a horror story about bread that never became bread. The main problem seems to be murdered yeast.

Never make bread without a thermometer. You'll notice the modern recipes call for the yeast to be "proofed" in a little warmed liquid. Just make sure the liquid is around 85 degrees. The yeast needs warmth to grow, but heat will blow it away. Don't go by such admonitions as "warm to the touch" liquid. Use the thermometer.

I've boiled down years of bread baking into a simple starter recipe for two pretty decent white loaves. From it, all I do is adjust the ingredients slightly to create dozens of variations, from oat-groat to whole wheat.

BOILING POINT, JAN. 29, 1986 • Bish was an inveterate bread baker, often eschewing bagged bread for loaves that he made on his own. Always eager to enlist new members into his bread-bakers circle, he provided this basic recipe for getting started.

1 CUP MILK

1 CUP WATER

1 TEASPOON SUGAR

2 TABLESPOONS (OR PACKETS) YEAST

1 TABLESPOON ADDITIONAL SUGAR

2 TEASPOONS SALT

1/4 CUP OF MELTED BUTTER OR 1/8 CUP OIL

6 CUPS FLOUR

1 EGG WHITE

DUSTING OF SESAME OR POPPY SEEDS

Combine and heat to about 100 degrees a cup of milk and a cup of water. Pour off a half cup of this into a mixing cup and let it cool to 85 degrees. Then add a teaspoon of sugar (it feeds the yeast) and 2 tablespoons (or 2 packets) of yeast.

Put this in a warm place. In about 10 minutes, it should be foaming and double in size. That means the yeast is ready to work. If nothing happens, the yeast is dead, so try again.

While it's proofing, dump the remaining liquid into a big bowl, add a tablespoon of sugar, 2 teaspoons of salt and 1/4 cup of melted butter or an 1/8 cup of oil. Stir well, then add the proofed yeast.

Stir into this a cup of flour for 100 strokes. Then stir in more flour, cup-by-cup, as you continue to work the dough. Use your hands when the dough gets too tough for a wooden spoon.

Transfer the dough to a floured surface. One of those large plastic cutting boards works well. Keep dusting on the flour until the stickiness ends. You'll probably use around 6 cups of flour in all. Then, for 10 minutes, knead the dough by hand. The dough will be ready when it is satiny smooth and rolls up without sticking to the board.

For the yeast to work and the flavor of the bread to ripen, you'll need to let it rise. Wash and dry your mixing bowl. Coat it with vegetable oil or butter. Roll the dough ball around in it to coat it, and cover it with wax paper.

Find a warm place for the rising. In the warm oven of a gas range with a pilot light is fine, or by a register. Don't let it get too hot. From 70 to 80 degrees is perfect.

The yeast will grow, creating gas on the way, which pushes up the dough. Depending on the temperature, the dough should double in bulk in an hour or two. When it doubles, punch it down and let it rise until it doubles a second time.

Finally, grease two bread pans and punch down the dough again. Knead it for another 5 to 10 minutes. Then divide it between the bread pans. Cover with the wax paper and let it rise until the bread is above the pan edges.

For a shiny top, brush the loaves with egg white before baking. This will allow you to dust them with sesame or poppy seeds.

The baking is simple. Heat your oven to 400 degrees. Bake the loaves at that temperature for 10 minutes and then back it off and bake at 375 for another 20 minutes.

Finally, take the loaves out of the pan and put them naked (the bread, not you) back into the oven for 5 minutes or so with the heat off to crisp the crusts. Remove and allow to cool slowly on a wire rack.

Now keep your hands off the loaves until they cool. Bread right from the oven isn't very pleasant.

Indeed, all this does take time. Is it worth it? I don't know about you, but the routine of my life rarely approaches nirvana, except on bread day.

FAT TUESDAY
WHAT BETTER TIME FOR LOOK AT BAYOU COOKING

LOCAL FIREFIGHTERS CAN RELAX, SOMEWHAT.

The blast of Louisiana Cajun cooking that seared our area—along with most of the Western eating world—three years ago has slackened to a simmer.

Chef Paul Prudhomme has gone back to marketing cheap spices with expensive prices. We see some lingering commercial fallout, the most common of which is really common: "Cajun" potato chips. Some yum.

The tendency is to write it all off and wait for the next binge of a food fad. But, like most food trends, this one leaves impressions, even if we no longer feel driven to risk self-immolation while trying to blacken a whitefish. (Or is it whiten a blackfish?)

Cajun New Orleans Louisiana cooking, whatever that is, has been compared to "fine French cuisine served on a sledgehammer." That sledgehammer can be enough cayenne pepper and garlic in one dish to last you a month. It's also a stereotype. Most dishes served in New Orleans non-touristy eater-

Jambalaya

Dirty rice, or jambalaya, has become an art form hereabouts. It fits perfectly with the move into whole grains. It is a refrigerator godsend, as you can use almost anything in it.

Rice terrorizes a lot of people for no good reason. For this dish, put 4 cups of chicken stock or bouillon into a saucepan along with 2 cups of raw, long-grain rice. Add two bay leaves and a whole garlic clove. Bring to a boil, then lower to a simmer and cook 15 minutes. Remove the clove.

Chop a medium onion and a 1/4-pound each of chicken livers and gizzards, or use chicken or turkey if you don't like organ meat. Brown this in some bacon drippings, adding a clove of chopped garlic, a cup of chopped green onions (tops included) and a 1/4 cup of chopped, fresh parsley. You could add chopped green or red peppers.

Combine all this stuff with the partially cooked rice in an oiled casserole dish. Add strips of 2-minute parboiled bacon on top. Cook uncovered in a 350-degree oven for 20 minutes or until the bacon browns.

If you want to spice this, load on the red pepper, hot sauce and a dusting of thyme. Put on as much as you think you can take. However, it's fine without any of the seasoning heat.

ies are mild. In New Orleans, it's the preparation, not necessarily the spices, that make the food.

The city's food has been influenced more by what happens in the backwaters of the Mississippi than by its French ancestry. Out there in the bayou, food is simple and unpretentious. It often reflects the poverty of the area (lack of meat, use of gizzards and such).

Spicy cooking almost always is a tip-off of economic conditions. People initially used a lot of spices to cover up the taste of spoiled food.

All of this, along with an amazing collection of river and sea foods as close as a fishnet or line, makes for some unusual and quite

LIFESTYLE FEATURE, JAN. 11, 1989 • When he wanted to, Jim could light a fire under area cooks, teaching them how to add warmth to their particular taste. These recipes, from the Deep South, were aimed at readers who wanted to add just a little spice to their culinary lives.

Shrimp Rice

Louisiana shrimp rice is great stuff, especially if you're faced with stretching a little bit of shrimp among a lot of people.

In a heavy skillet, brown a cup of rice in a film of hot oil. Browned rice shouldn't be dark brown—just a trifle brown, enough to toast up the flavor and make it nutty. Keep stirring it.

Then add a diced, medium onion, or 1/2 cup of shallots if you have them. Next comes 1/4 cup of finely diced celery hearts. Pour into this 1/2 quart of tomato sauce, adding a dash of cayenne and hot sauce and salt to taste. Cover and let it simmer slowly. Check every 15 minutes and add tomato sauce if it's getting too dry.

Peel and devein a dozen fresh, green shrimp and wash thoroughly. When the rice is done, place the shrimp atop it, dust with cayenne and cover tightly. Lower heat to a hint. In 5 minutes or so, the shrimp will be steamed done and very tender.

pleasant eating. Leave the titles of "Cajun" or "New Orleans-style" at home. Down there, it's just daily food, if you're fortunate enough to find the real thing.

It's also simple to prepare, and that perks up the ears of cooks as far north as here. If you want a quick meal with a potential for raves, try Louisiana.

JIM'S CALZONES
Some assembly required

CALZONE? STROMBOLI? THEY SOUND LIKE THE ITALIAN FAMILY DOWN THE STREET. THAT'S THE PROBLEM WITH A NAME.

Call them what they are—turnovers—and many Americans would discover them. Of course, the Italians down the street would have something to say about that name change. A turnover to them is a giro d'affari. OK, let's stick with calzones and stromboli.

I'm convinced that Italian cuisine is the most frugal in the world, and calzones and stromboli confirm this. You take some scrap dough from your bread making and roll it into a circle. Then add leftover meats, cheeses, veggies or anything else in the fridge. Fold the dough in half, seal the edges and bake. That's it, ready to grace a dinner plate with a side of tomato sauce or a lunch bucket on its own.

These turnovers, for some odd reason, are hard to find. I'd think every pizza shop would offer them because they already have the ingredients, but no. It's that "some assembly required" that kills them.

Pizza Hut recently took the plunge. Well, sort of. They offer a calzone derivative called a P'zone (a "PA zone," not a "peez on"). It's actually a 12-inch covered pizza for six bucks.

A calzone or stromboli to me looks a lot like a single-serving turnover (not an egg roll or a giant ravioli, thank you) and always has a surprise inside. Meat and cheese are the main ingredients, but the world is your oyster, and they're good in there, too.

I made some the other day with bacon, pepperoni, ham, Swiss and mozzarella cheeses and sun-dried tomatoes (whew), a calzone Dagwood. They were a home run.

The problem with calzones is the dough, and this stops a lot of folks from making them. Almost all recipes call for simple pizza dough or

BOILING POINT, FEB. 27, 2002 • The range of Jim Hillibish's culinary skills included a diversity of ethnic origins. One of his favorite styles of cooking was Italian, and he passed it on with a "Little Italy" kind of spirit that was enough to warm your heart no matter what your cultural background.

that unbaked, frozen bread dough from the store.

Shaping this stuff into a circle and then stretching it over your ingredients is bad news. It tears, flops around and acts like it's never going to work. It takes about six hands to do it right, then it pulls apart in the oven, welding the cheese onto your poor baking sheet.

One magical day, I made a bad mistake with the dough and solved the problem forever. Instead of a tablespoon of olive oil, I dumped in a quarter cup. Talk about a brain burp.

OK, I never throw anything away without giving it a chance, so I kneaded the dough and rolled it out to a quarter-inch thick. Then I noticed something. Instead of acting goofy, the dough just sat there. It had enough elasticity not to tear on folding, and it stuck together perfectly.

With all this oil, you do need a wash of egg whites before baking to get a nice browning. I painted it on with a pastry brush.

End result: Perfect calzones, all beautiful; and no cheese leaks. The dough was the best ever, delicious and without that "big-bready" flavor of pizza dough.

It must have been a good day for me, because I solved the dough-cutting problem at the same time. I grabbed a 5-inch diameter sauce-pot lid and cut the circles with it in the rolled dough. Then I re-rolled them back to a quarter inch thick. Why did I never think of this before?

Bake your calzones on an olive-oiled cookie sheet or on a pizza brick and cornmeal. Serve hot and warn your guests the filling will burn.

These freeze well, so make a bunch, ready for a meal in a microwave minute. They're perfect for brown bagging, a one-handed snack at the ballpark or on picnics. Wrap in foil and a towel, and they will stay warm for hours in an insulated container.

If you're not eating them soon, place them frozen in your lunch box and then nuke them at work.

A traditional Italian calzone has a ricotta cheese filling (15 ounces of ricotta makes four; mix with a half cup of Parmesan and a teaspoon of basil). Use this as a starting point or invent your own.

One thing to remember is raw meats such as ground beef, sausage, chicken and bacon must be browned ahead.

I used to think that a calzone primarily was cheese, and a stromboli (which is an active volcano in Italy) was mostly meat and veggies. That doesn't hold up any more. Seems like the two have merged.

The other must is to invite your Italian neighbors over as the beautiful aroma of baking goodies wafts down the street.

For the dough

1 1/3 CUPS WARM WATER
1/4 CUP OLIVE OIL (NOT YOUR BEST STUFF)
1 TEASPOON SALT
1 TEASPOON DRIED OREGANO
4 CUPS ALL-PURPOSE FLOUR
2 1/2 TEASPOONS REGULAR YEAST

Mix ingredients in order in your bread machine (dough setting) or by hand. Allow to rise in the machine for an hour or in a warm place in a bowl covered with oiled plastic wrap and a towel. Punch down and allow to rise again for another hour.

Roll out to a quarter-inch thick on a floured board. Cut with the rim of a 5-inch diameter pot lid. Roll again to a quarter inch, add ingredients in the center and seal. Run a fork around the edges to complete the sealing. Brush on egg whites.

Bake on a cookie sheet spread with olive oil or cornmeal. Preheat oven to 400 degrees and bake 20 to 25 minutes or until nicely browned.

Makes 5 to 6 calzones.

For the filling

Generally, it's meat and cheese, but it could be all vegetable or combinations of just about anything. If you use ricotta, divide 12 ounces among four calzones. Add 1 or 2 tablespoons of mozzarella to each.

A vegetarian calzone includes spinach in the ricotta. The spinach should be chopped and dry. Mushrooms are nice.

If making meatball calzones, use small, browned meatballs and a thin layer of tomato sauce. Add mozzarella or goat cheese or both.

If I use ricotta, I add Italian herbs such as basil or oregano to the cheese, plus Parmesan or romano grated cheese. Ricotta by itself is too bland for me.

Remember Dick's coney sauce?

Food memories. Can we ever really go back? It's a tough order.

Readers have sent me a dozen different recipes, each purporting to make the original coney sauce served at Dick's Sandwich Shop in the old Arcade Market downtown.

Frankly, I thought Dick's was good, but the coneys at the Golden Pheasant two blocks east on East Tusc were the best downtown. I hate to mention this. I know it will set off yet another coney war.

Anyway, do we really remember exactly what food tasted like 40 years ago? Be honest now. I doubt it.

We do remember Dick's, an always-friendly place jammed with downtowners needing a 10-minute lunch. But as for the coney sauce, well, perhaps we remember it just as being good.

Part of this is due to food changes. Hot dogs definitely are different today, lower in fat. The ground beef in Dick's sauce was different from today's. Ours is a lot leaner, and probably made from lower-quality beef. The tomato puree was different, too. So was the chili powder. The result is we cannot really duplicate Dick's sauce, even if we could identify it after all these decades.

The other part is our taste buds have changed, too. The older you get, the fewer you have. This is why children cannot tolerate spicy foods. Their tastes are too acute for it. It's also why many folks say food tasted much better when they were young. So, even if we duplicated the Dick's sauce exactly, it still will not taste the same as when we ate it years ago.

The latest alleged Dick's recipe to arrive here at least has some pedigree. It's from Danny Wadsworth, whose Coney Days at Timken's Gambrinus Bearing Plant are still remembered by his buddies. I'll take four, with onions and mustard.

The wife of one of Danny's friends worked at Dick's for years. She preserved the sauce recipe when he closed.

This one does look like a restaurant sauce. It has only four ingredients, making it cheap, easy and fast. It has a lot of sugar, and I do recall Dick's sauce was sweet. It makes a lot, enough for at least 6 pounds of hot dogs.

Throw a coney party and give it a try. I'd bet it brings back memories, whatever they are. It sure did for me.

BOILING POINT, FEB. 9, 2005 • Jim had a history in Canton and knew where the city's culinary traditions were born. The recipes for many of them appeared in his writing over the years, such as this fondly remembered downtown lunch treat.

Arcade Market Coney Sauce

3 POUNDS GROUND BEEF (DANNY USES FISHERS STANDARD GROUND BEEF)

1/3 CUP CHILI POWDER (REGULAR, NOT HOT) • 1/2 CUP SUGAR (SOUNDS LIKE A LOT, BUT IT'S CORRECT)

1 GALLON TOMATO PUREE (RED PACK BRAND)

Brown the beef in an 8-quart non-reactive pot, mashing the chunks into fine pieces with a spatula. Drain off fat and liquid. Reduce heat to medium and stir in chili powder. Add tomato puree and stir all.

Reduce heat to low and stir in the sugar. Simmer over low heat for 30 minutes.

Serve with mustard and onions on the side. Steam the buns.

NOTE: Cut ingredients in half to make a more manageable size. The sauce freezes well.

HOW MANY SLIDERS CAN YOU EAT?

I'M AT WHITE CASTLE. I'VE JUST FINISHED SIX CHEESE SLIDERS AND GO TO THE COUNTER TO ORDER SOME TAKEOUT. I LOOK AT THE LITTLE GIRL NAMED "HELLO I'M MANDY" IN THE EYE AND WHISPER:

"OK, how do they make these puppies?"

She just stares at me as her brain does a database sort on that company policy lecture she attended last year. Apparently, we have a file not found.

"It's a secret, I think," she says.

I love it when they say that. It gets my dormant investigative-reporter genes raving. So I arrive home with my little burgers and do a quick Google on "White Castle recipe." Three-hundred-and-forty-two-thousand hits. One suspects the secret is, uh, no more.

Walt Anderson would cringe. In 1921, he became the contrarian of a revolution. Beef suddenly was out, way out. Upton Sinclair's novel on meatpacking, "The Jungle," grossed out everybody. It was so well written, it seemed like fact. It harmed the beef industry for years. Especially maligned was hamburger. Nobody would touch it. Walt took it on himself to rebuild beef's reputation. He created White Castle Hamburgers, the first fast-food chain. He figured the whole thing was cleanliness, and his restaurants remain spotless. He also needed to get the price down to a nickel. His burgers today remain stuck at 2.5 inches square on a little dinner roll.

Hence their nickname—sliders. They're so small, they slide down to a happy landing in Mr. Tummy. And you cannot eat just one or two.

White Castle's sliders have become the most imitated burgers on the planet. They're a hit everywhere, except McDonald's, which clings to the bigger

BOILING POINT, FEB. 2, 2010 • Reproducing favorite foods from restaurants of our past is a common game for cooks. One of Jim's fond memories was of dining on the small sandwiches he found at White Castle, and when he returned home, he tried to duplicate them.

Slider Heaven

2 POUNDS GROUND BEEF

2 TABLESPOONS WATER

2 EGGS

1 LARGE ONION, FINELY DICED

1 TEASPOON SALT

Spread the onion thinly on a 9-by-13-inch cookie sheet with raised edges. Mix the meat with remaining ingredients and spread in a thin layer over the onions. Poke holes with a fork every two inches. Bake 20-25 minutes at 400 degrees. Place cheese slices on top to melt before serving.

Cut into 2 1/2-inch-square burgers and serve with dill pickle slices on Pepperidge Farm small dinner rolls. Makes 18 to 20.

Alternative way: Omit the salt and add an envelope of onion-soup mix to the above. Form meat into 20 small balls. Flatten on a greased cookie sheet with sides (no extra onions). Bake as indicated.

White Castle Sliders

1 1/2 POUNDS 80 PERCENT GROUND BEEF

1 1/4 OUNCES ONION SOUP MIX • 1 EGG • 1 MEDIUM ONION, DICED

FRESHLY GROUND BLACK PEPPER TO TASTE • 24 SLIDER OR DINNER ROLLS

Mix onion soup mix, ground beef and pepper. Press into a lightly oiled cookie sheet to the raised edges. Poke holes in the meat with a fork and press diced onion into the meat. Bake for 10 to 15 minutes at 400. Turn off heat and add American cheese slices to melt. Warm dinner rolls at the same time. Cut meat into 24 squares. Serve on rolls. Top with dill pickle slices. Serve with mustard and ketchup. Makes 24.

the better thing.

I love sliders. You can order and consume just enough. These are small, but the most tasty use of ground beef.

Good sliders are everywhere: Corner bars, yuppie chains, family-style sit-downs and Bloomingdale's David Burke restaurant in Manhattan ($14.50 for three).

As for the secret recipes, they take some digestion. The onion-soup thing is a replacement for the real stuff. Onion is the primary slider flavor. It's part of the big secret. They cook the burgers on a bed of onions.

Anway, here's the revisionist thinking on WC sliders baking burgers.

WHITE SAUCE

FROM SCRATCH IS WORTH THE TIME INVOLVED

YOU WILL BE TEMPTED TO REACH FOR THE MUSHROOM-SOUP CAN ON THIS. DON'T YOU DARE. YOU WILL MISS A WHITE-SAUCE MASTERPIECE.

Crafting an elegant white sauce is a cooking fundamental. It's an important part of dozens of recipes. Think where you need a white sauce. The short list:

Pasta Alfredo, Swedish meatballs, macaroni and cheese, chicken and noodles, broiled fish, steamed vegetables of all manner, all cream soups and casseroles by the mile.

Learning this sauce gives you a lifetime of dishes surprisingly better tasting than those made with canned soup. It's worth the effort.

You'll make three basic types. Thin goes into soups. Thick smothers croquettes and biscuits. Medium is all-purpose. The only difference between them is the amount of milk or cream.

Most of these sauces are made from milk. Cream will be smoother and brighter white, but a fat disaster. I often compromise with half-and-half. The only reason to use white pepper is to avoid the specks of black.

You'll need a wire whisk or hand blender. That's important to inject air as it cooks. Remember too that sauces are delicate and burn fast. Keep whisking and keep the temperature on low. In the old days when stoves were not as adjustable, they made these in double boilers.

I think white wine improves any white sauce, but that's optional. In sauces with cheese, you can increase the flavor by adding a dash of wine vinegar.

BOILING POINT, FEB. 24, 2009 • "Keep It Simple" was one of Jim Hillibish's mantras. A lot of delicious sophisticated dishes could be concocted from an otherwise uncomplicated central ingredient, as this recipe for Bish's special sauce will show.

2 TABLESPOONS BUTTER OR MARGARINE

2 TABLESPOONS FLOUR • 1 TEASPOON SALT

1/4 TEASPOON WHITE PEPPER • 1/4 CUP WHITE WINE (OPTIONAL)

2 CUPS MILK, HALF AND HALF OR CREAM (APPROX.)

Melt the butter in a saucepan. Add flour, salt and pepper and whisk until flour combines with butter. (This is a roux.) Slowly add your liquid choice and wine while whisking or using an electrical blending stick to dissolve all lumps. As the sauce thickens, add more liquid until it is the consistency you want. Then cook on low for 10 minutes stirring often to prevent burning.

Use the above to create the following:

Cheese Sauce

Skip the wine, add 1/2 cup shredded cheddar or Swiss cheese and a teaspoon of mustard and 1/2 teaspoon of vinegar.

Steamed Vegetables

Add 1 tablespoon mayonnaise and one teaspoon of freshly ground lemon juice or vinegar. Or use cheese sauce.

Alfredo Pasta

Add 2 cloves of minced garlic, a half cup of grated mozzarella cheese and 1/4 cup of grated Parmesan cheese.

Meatballs/Noodles

Add 1/2 cup sliced, sautéed mushrooms, 1/4 teaspoon dried tarragon.

Soups

Add 2 teaspoons of chicken-broth powder or 2 cubes of chicken bouillon. You may need to dilute with more liquid.

Creamed Chicken

Brown chicken in butter and remove. Add flour to chicken skillet to make the roux. Add liquid and whisk in 2 beaten egg yolks pouring slowly on low heat, cook thoroughly. For paprikash, whisk in 1/4 cup of sour cream at the end and 1/2 teaspoon of paprika.

Beef Stroganoff

Add a beef bouillon cube and 1/2 teaspoon of celery seed. Add meat and sautéed onions. At the end, stir in 3 tablespoons of sour cream.

HOW TO FIX A SAUCE

White sauces containing eggs and mayonnaise can suddenly separate on the stove resulting in a grainy texture. This is called breaking. If this happens, whisk or blend an egg yolk in a bowl and add a teaspoon of cold water. Then pour the sauce into the egg yolk slowly while whisking rapidly. Then continue cooking. This works in most cases.

Sauces containing sour cream can break, too. Add the sour cream at the end and warm but do not boil.

Soothing soup

It's economical, nourishing, versatile and easy to make

NO KIDDING, THEY'VE RESEARCHED THIS: WHEN YOU'RE LONELY, SICK AND YOU WANT YOUR MOMMY, SOUP IS THE NEXT BEST THING.

Soup is rated as the No. 1 comfort food, more comforting, even, than marshmallows.

We all remember being bedfast with the sore throats of youth that suddenly got better after we heard the morning school bus pass. We stayed in bed anyway. We knew mom soon would be up there with a lap tray and a cup filled with soothing soup.

Many food historians believe that's how soup got its start—nourishment for cave persons who on a bad day just couldn't stomach another stegosaurus steak.

Soup is comfortable in hard times, too. Nothing's more economical. Nothing else will stretch a forlorn chicken breast between a family of four. Soup got us through the Depression, through cash-short college days, through 15 percent mortgage rates.

Soup remains the cheapest meal in the store. You still can get a can of tomato for a quarter, a package of dried ramen noodle soup for even less. Likewise, soup remains one of the least understood of foods.

If you reach for the can opener each time your family demands soup, you're making a mistake. Canned soups have improved greatly over the years, but they're still, uh, canned. That means overcooked vegetables, melded instead of distinctive flavors and a general ho-hum to it all. They're OK perhaps for a fast lunch, but nothing to start off a full-course beef Wellington feast.

Canned soup takes its lumps with the anti-sodium crowd. A lot of its flavor comes from added salt.

So what's a cook to do? Make it.

Your own soup making can be straightforward, unpretentious and quite easy. Forget the images of yesteryear, with giant cauldrons simmering for days on wood stoves. With some advance work, you're set for months of fresh homemade in a little more time than it takes to warm a mundane can.

Here's a tour de force of fresh, basic soup. Use the stock for creating your own recipes. It's almost impossible to mess up. Don't wait for a sore throat or homesickness to make some.

FOOD FEATURE, FEB. 22, 1989 • Inexpensive foods that were simple to make and comforting to eat—but nourishing for a body seeking weapons to fight off an illness—were important to Jim Hillibish when he was concocting a recipe for nature's cures. And to Jim, it all started with a basic soup stock.

Turkey Rice Soup

2/3 CUP UNCOOKED RICE • 3 1/2 CUPS BROTH • 3 1/2 CUPS WATER • 4 CUPS COARSELY CHOPPED, COOKED TURKEY

1 CUP DIAGONALLY SLICED CELERY • 4 MEDIUM CARROTS CUT INTO MATCH STICKS

2 CUPS MIXED FRESH VEGETABLES (YOUR CHOICE OF DICED BROCCOLI, MUSHROOMS, BAMBOO SHOOTS, WATER CHESTNUTS, SNOW PEAS, SWEET PEPPER, WHATEVER)

2 TABLESPOONS DRY SHERRY • 2 TABLESPOONS LOW-SODIUM SOY SAUCE • 1 1/2 TEASPOONS CORNSTARCH

This is soup-making with an Oriental flavor. Feel free to substitute chicken for turkey. Use just about any fresh vegetables you have on hand. The wine and soy sauce really make the dish.

Combine the rice, broth and water in a 4-quart saucepan. Bring to a boil and cook for 10 minutes. Add fresh vegetables, cover and cook for 15 minutes or until tender. Add turkey and simmer for 5 minutes. Combine remaining ingredients and stir into broth. Simmer, stirring, until soup is clear and slightly thickened. Serve garnished with sliced scallions, including the green tops. This makes 10 servings and freezes well.

Making Stock

It's the most important thing. What you put in it is up to the leftovers in your fridge.

Canned beef or chicken stock is not bad in a time pinch, mainly because you or the canning people can't overcook the stuff. But it, too, will have extra salt plus some "flavor enhancers" that you'd never put in there on your own.

Fresh stock is simpler but takes time. So make a lot and freeze it for easy using any other time. It's economical. You make it from bones you'd be throwing out if it weren't soup day.

Resist your dog's urgings and make a habit of saving bones. Any kind will do—chicken or turkey carcasses, beef or port, fresh or cooked, in any combination. Keep a bag of them in the freezer and keep adding to them.

When you get about 5 pounds, load them into a big pot. Add 2 medium onions studded with cloves, 4 whole cloves of garlic, 6 carrots sliced lengthwise, 4 bay leaves, a handful of whole peppercorns, the top leaves and outer ribs of 6 stalks of celery and 10 or more parsley stalks, plus salt. Actually, anything goes here. Raid your veggie keeper. Soup is the great consumer of things past their prime.

Cover all of this with cold water, about 10 quarts. Bring to a boil. Skim off the foam, reduce heat and cover. It should just be simmering. Let it cook all afternoon, 4 or 5 hours will do.

An hour before you turn off the heat, throw in a whole chicken (3 to 4 pounds) and beef brisket (3 pounds will do). Cook until the meat is tender. One can be supper one night and the other supper the next night.

Finally, strain the broth into quart containers. By now, you'll probably have 6 or 7 quarts. Refrigerate overnight. Next morning, skim off the congealed fat. Then freeze. You're now set for months of easy soup-making.

(Whew.) Or use canned broth.

Cucumber Soup

This takes 15 minutes. It's also a grand dish, perfect to begin a fancy meal or just Sunday supper.

Heat a quart of stock. Peel, quarter and seed 2 cucumbers. Cut crosswise into pieces an eighth of an inch wide. Make a small cut in the top of each piece. Cook in the stock for 10 minutes or until the cucumber is slightly tender. You can add some diced scallions or parsley or chives just before serving.

Pea Soup

This is far from that pasty stuff you associate with the name.

Heat a quart of stock. Throw in 1/2 pound of well-washed, fresh sugar peas with stems and strings removed, still in the pods. Make sure they're fresh, new peas in tender pods. Simmer until the pods are tender. Remove the pods and shell them. Put the peas into the soup and simmer until the peas are done. Float a slice of lemon on each bowlful.

Beef & Barley Soup

Get that quart of stock simmering. Add a pound or so of cubed stew meat you've browned in advance. Boil, skim the surface, then cover and cook for an hour. Add 1/4 cup of pearl barley and 1/4 cup of rice, plus 2 cups of stewed tomatoes, a sliced onion and freshly ground pepper. Cook for an hour.

Skim the fat from top before serving, or make it a day ahead, chill and scrape off the congealed fat before reheating.

SALMON EN PAPILLOTE
Fish won't be parched with parchment

IN MY LEARNING DAYS OF COOKING, I OFTEN BOUGHT TWICE THE AMOUNT OF FISH I NEEDED BECAUSE I JUST KNEW I'D OVERCOOK IT THE FIRST TIME.

A lot of you out there share my fear. Many folks shun home-cooked seafood.

One of my nurses at the dialysis center was moaning that she felt guilty she wasn't feeding her family fish, but she knew she'd blow the cooking every time. She needed a way to prepare it that works every time, guaranteed. She needed an old French concept, cooking in paper.

That sounds like a disaster in the making. Won't the paper catch fire in the heat of the oven? Won't the juices drip through? Won't the fish taste like, you know, paper?

Not if you search the corners of your grocery for a box of baking parchment. You'll probably have to ask a stocker for it.

Parchment, as ancient writers knew, is hard, almost permanent paper that stands up against anything, including heat and moisture. It's perfect for cooking because it insulates your delicate ingredients against the hellfire of the oven.

The French, whose cuisine cannot tolerate overcooking, long ago discovered this paper has a use beyond the Dead Sea scrolls. They use more cooking parchment than any others. The parchment you buy here often is made in France.

They call it cooking en papillote, for "in paper." It's a lifesaver, and it works with any baked dish recipe.

I know, you're wondering why not just cover the fish in a pan and bake away. Even if you do this, chances are that the bottom of the fish will be overdone due to contact with the hot pan. Do it in parchment and the insulation solves that nasty problem.

Parchment seals the steam of the food next to its surface. That means it's injected back into the food, boosting flavor instead of burning it off. Those French know their stuff.

My drill is to add fresh herbs, such as tarragon, basil or rosemary, to the package. I dribble on a little white wine and place thin lemon slices or zest on top. Then I tightly wrap the package and place it on a wire rack in a baking pan.

Depending on the thickness of the fish, it usually takes 20 minutes at 375 degrees. When I unwrap the

BOILING POINT, FEB. 21, 2001 • Cooking "en papillote"—it was a French concept. Bish told readers in plain English to cook their fish "in paper" —not his newspaper, but rather in parchment—if they did not want it to overcook.

2 TEASPOONS EXTRA VIRGIN OLIVE OIL, DIVIDED

1 MEDIUM CARROT, CUT IN LONG MATCHSTICKS

1 MEDIUM ZUCCHINI, CUT IN LONG MATCHSTICK PIECES

1 MEDIUM LEEK OR ONION, SLICED THINLY

1/4 CUP WATER

4 TEASPOONS DRY WHITE WINE, SUCH AS VERMOUTH

1 TABLESPOON EACH MINCED FRESH DILL AND LEMON JUICE

1 TEASPOON EACH GRATED LEMON PEEL AND DIJON-STYLE MUSTARD

1/4 TEASPOON SEA SALT

1/8 TEASPOON WHITE PEPPER

2 SALMON STEAKS (6 OUNCES EACH)

In a 10-inch skillet, heat 1 teaspoon of oil over medium high heat. Add vegetables and sauté until slightly tender, 3 to 4 minutes. Stir in remaining ingredients except fish and oil. Cook, stirring occasionally, for 2 minutes. Preheat oven to 375 degrees. Using pastry brush, grease centers of 2 15-inch long pieces of parchment with 1/2 teaspoon of oil each.

Place salmon steak on center of each sheet. Spoon half of vegetable mixture and liquid over each steak. Fold paper over steaks to enclose, crimping edges to seal.

Place packets on a wire rack in a baking pan. Bake for 20 minutes (until salmon separates easily when tested with a fork and vegetables are tender). Carefully remove salmon and vegetables intact to warm serving plates.

Makes 2 servings.

package, well, that first whiff is heaven.

Fish cooked this way is more solid, not that falling apart stuff we've come to know and dread. The flavorings you've added penetrate deeply and do not lose their bright quality. Many restaurants use this technique, and that's how they cook tons of fish to perfection.

I gave the following recipe to nurse Vicki, and she can't stop talking about it. It works well with any type of fish, but salmon is my favorite. It's a meal in paper. Incidentally, you could use foil instead of parchment, but I don't think the French would approve.

BRINGING A FRESHNESS TO FOOD

A sour surprise in bread baking

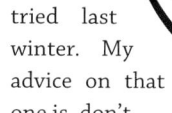

GOOFY BUT GREAT ALWAYS SCARES ME. SAUERKRAUT BREAD IS ABOUT AS SCARY AS IT GETS.

This little dance down Goofy Lane begins on bread-making day at our house. I'm really tired of SOS bread (same old stuff): Mix it, knead it, bake it, throw out half of it to the squirrels after it molds.

We need something different. I see some ancient, stone-ground rye flour in a corner of the fridge. OK, rye bread it is.

As I pull the flour bag out of the fridge, I notice there's a canning jar of sauerkraut in back of it, a remnant of last summer's homemade krautmania that made our basement smell like an open sewer for three months. I look at it. It looks at me. I grab it.

Sudden urges to dump sauerkraut into raw bread dough can prove insanity in court. It makes as much sense as adding grape Jell-O to dinner-roll dough ("We won't need any jelly"), which I tried last winter. My advice on that one is, don't.

Why would a sober baker even fantasize about sauerkraut in bread? If you take a deep breath and think about it, there are some pluses. Sourdough rye is famous. Sauerkraut is sour.

About half of the rye bread in the country is wrapped around corned beef, and half of that has a big dollop of sauerkraut on top, with Swiss cheese and Thousand Island dressing. That's a Reuben, and it's pretty good. Why not prepackage the sauerkraut taste? No more drippy fingers. What a long shot.

So I'm laying out my ingredients, and Kathleen pops in for a handful of ginger snaps. She looks at the sauerkraut next to my bread bowl, and she looks at me.

"You're not ..."

"Just go read the paper and forget you've seen this."

If I had any intention of not dumping sauerkraut into bread dough, this little exchange ended it. I'm now in it for the duration, come hell or cabbage-stringy breakfast toast.

That was my big worry. Cabbage over high heat tends to toughen. I like chewy bread, but this might be ridiculous.

Anyway, I strained a cup of kraut. We don't need that extra liquid. Then I chopped it finely, praying this would cure the strings.

Then I followed my usual ryedough recipe, including brown sugar, molasses and the all-important caraway seeds. I felt good about the tablespoon of caraway. I always use it in sauerkraut. Finally, some sense creeps into this recipe.

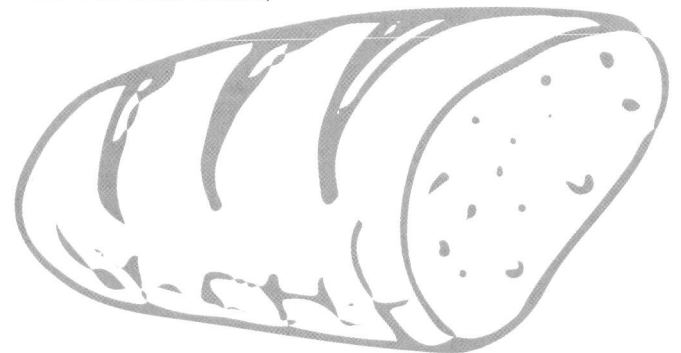

BOILING POINT, MARCH 27, 2002 • How did Jim Hillibish come up with this choice recipe for Sour Dough Rye Bread? Well, the secret ingredient, which nearly disappears in the baking of the bread, is sauerkraut.

Sour (Kraut) Dough Rye Bread

1 CUP JUST-WARM MILK

2 CUPS WHITE FLOUR

1 CUP RYE FLOUR (STONE GROUND IS NICE)

2 TABLESPOONS BROWN SUGAR

2 TABLESPOONS DARK MOLASSES

1 TEASPOON SALT

1 1/2 TABLESPOONS BUTTER

1 TABLESPOON CARAWAY SEEDS

1 CUP SAUERKRAUT, DRAINED, FINELY CHOPPED

1 1/2 TEASPOONS POWDERED YEAST

If you're making this in a bread machine, add the ingredients in the order listed and use the Whole Wheat, Large setting.

By hand, proof the yeast in the warm milk until it bubbles. Mix the other ingredients in a large bowl by hand or with a mixer. Add the yeast and mix and knead until the dough is satiny. You may need to add a little more white flour depending on how wet your sauerkraut is.

Cover and allow to rise for an hour in a warm place. Punch down and knead for another 10 minutes. Shape into a ball and place on a corn-meal-sprinkled baking sheet or pizza brick. Brush the ball with milk.

Bake 30 minutes at 400 degrees, checking for doneness at 25 minutes. The loaf is done when it sounds hollow when rapped. Cool on a wire rack.

Yield: One 1 1/2-pound loaf.

I decided on a free-form loaf and balled it up on my pizza brick, spread with corn meal. I painted it with milk and let her rip in the oven at 400 degrees.

Soon, the kitchen filled with the aroma of a fine Reuben. Notice I'm not using the word stink. All that was missing was a heap of corned beef.

I couldn't wait until the loaf cooled to take a knife to it. First thing I noticed: The sauerkraut had disappeared. Second thing: Wow, this is really good stuff.

So I'm suggesting you try it. Don't tell anybody you're doing it. Just take the plunge, and enjoy the shrieks of surprise when they taste it.

This, by the way, would be great for one of those ubiquitous bread bowls of spinach dip at every party in town. It also makes wunderbar fried croutons for salads and soups. I guarantee none of the loaf will got to the squirrels.

MANNING UP QUICHE
ADD PECS APPEAL TO THE 'Q' WORD TO MAKE MANLY MEAL

I ABSOLUTELY HATE BRUCE FEIRSTEIN. HIS CULT EPIC "REAL MEN DON'T EAT QUICHE" CLOSED THE BOOK ON A DECENT BREAKFAST FOR ALL OF US MENFOLK.

It was so nice. We'd get up early and concoct a beautiful pie of eggs and cheese and anything else from the fridge.

It was so easy, even a man could do it. Then our wives would awaken to a wonderful repast and not bother us about chores or football for the rest of the day. Heaven.

These days, the only place you'll find quiche is in female restaurants. No man has eaten quiche since the Feirstein slam closed our minds way back in 1982.

Instead, menfolk stand over the sink inhaling a bowl of cereal and call it breakfast. Sometimes it isn't even that good. It's a tepid toaster bagel and a gulp of milk straight from the carton. We eat many of our breakfasts one-handed in our cars or at the vending machines at work. It sucks rubber doughnuts.

I'm thinking it's time to take a gulp and test our masculinity with a slice of warm quiche.

Will we turn into sissy cats in frilly aprons? Bet we don't.

Perhaps all we need is to change the name of the dish. Quiche sounds pretty fem, anyway. How about Pectoral Pie or Linebacker Lather?

The essence of this dish centers on four eggs, sometimes separated, sometimes simply scrambled. Anything else you throw in there is up to you. If you use veggies or meats, sauté them beforehand. They won't bake long enough to cook on their own.

You could add cheese on top or mix it in with the eggs, or do both (better). Cheese is an important part of the dish, and very manly, I might add.

Feel free to change this dish in any way.

Nice spice combos are chili pepper and cumin for Mexican, tarragon and/or dill for French, and basil and oregano for Italian.

If a pie crust is woman's work in your house, forget it. Bake your Pectoral Pie directly in a greased pie pan.

The original P.P. (I can't believe I wrote that) was Swiss cheese and mushroom.

Extra cheese was grated on top and browned for a minute under the broiler.

More manly versions include precooked sausage, bacon (or both). And anchovies. Don't forget the stinkin' anchovies.

The only trick is to be sure to partially bake the crust (about half the time of fully baked).

This keeps the crust from getting soggy. Soggy is no good for any gender.

Anyway, here's my favorite version. It has a lot of pecs appeal:

BOILING POINT, MARCH 7, 2001 • Bish kept a close eye on the trends—in both books and food. Sometimes, popular culture could be combined with popular culinary dishes, and Jim made the results interesting in a column.

Call It Quiche And He Won't Eat It Pie

1 9-INCH PIE CRUST, HALF BAKED

1/2 CUP CHOPPED BACON

1/4 CUP DICED RED ONIONS

1/4 CUP CHOPPED GREEN AND RED BELL PEPPERS

1/2 CUP SLICED MUSHROOMS

1 CLOVE MINCED GARLIC

2 POUNDS TOMATOES, PEELED, SEEDED AND DICED

1/2 TEASPOON BASIL

1/2 TEASPOON OREGANO

1/2 TEASPOON SALT

3 TABLESPOONS TOMATO PASTE

3 TABLESPOONS CHOPPED FRESH PARSLEY

1/8 TEASPOON FRESHLY GROUND BLACK PEPPER

4 LARGE EGGS (1 EGG AND 3 YOLKS)

1 1/2 CUPS MILK

12 BLACK OLIVES, SLICED

1/3 CUP GRATED PARMESAN CHEESE

8 ANCHOVY FILLETS (VERY OPTIONAL)

Pie crust should be partially baked. Use same oven temperature as for cooking quiche, 350 degrees, and time it so crust will bake about 4-7 minutes. Let it cool about 5 minutes before filling with mixture to continue baking.

Sauté bacon in a skillet until fat releases.

Add vegetables and seasonings, including parsley. Cover and cook over low heat for 5 minutes until tender.

Remove cover and raise heat so liquid evaporates.

Do not let mixture burn. Remove from heat.

Mix one egg and three egg yolks with milk and tomato paste. Combine with vegetable-bacon mixture and pour into crust.

Top with olives, grated cheese and (totally optional but manly) anchovies. Bake about 30 minutes or until firm and golden brown.

Serves six women, two men or one NFL linebacker.

BODACIOUS BLINTZES
Ready for breakfast

BLINTZES, THE TRA-DITIONAL FARE OF INNER-CITY DELI-CATESSENS, ARE MAK-ING A COMEBACK IN OUR OWN DOWNTOWN.

Tom Calhoun, owner-chef of A Deli of a Place at 333 Cleveland Avenue NW, says the crepe concoction, a staple in New York City, slowly is gaining converts here.

Tom, a graduate of the prestigious Culinary Institute of America, opened the small restaurant in September with an eye to offering something more than hamburgers.

On the menu are huge deli sandwiches, including a giant corned beef—and the McKinley Monument, an 11-ingredient submarine.

But for breakfast, amid the usual eggs and bacon, are the blintzes, deliciously light pancake wrappers served around fruits, sour cream, applesauce, cheese or just plain.

Tom likes a loose batter. It produces the thinnest of blintzes. He uses a traditional blintz-making utensil, a sort of upside-down pan which he heats to a sizzle over his gas fire and then dips the curved top into his blintz batter. A few minutes on the stove and the crepe easily is peeled off the top.

Blintzes may be made at home with the usual crepe pans, although they'll have to be turned. With a blintz-maker, there's no need to turn.

FEATURE, MARCH 26, 1986 • Tradition had a firmly entrenched place in Jim Hillibish's recipe box, and not all the recipes he shared with readers were his. Some were preserved by cooks in now-defunct restaurants, saved for posterity from an urban time long ago, and were shared with Bish … who fortunately for the rest of us couldn't keep them to himself.

1 1/4 CUPS FLOUR
PINCH OF SALT
1 1/2 CUPS MILK
2 TABLESPOONS OIL

Mix the above in a blender or stir well with a wire whip. Let the batter stand for an hour in the refrigerator to allow the flour's gluten to develop. Dip a hot blintz pan into the batter, or pour and spread a 1/4 cup of batter into a lightly oiled crepe pan and cook.

Cheese blintz filling

Blend 1 cup ricotta cheese or 3 ounces cream cheese with 2/3 cup of cottage cheese. Stir in sugar to taste, 1/2 teaspoon vanilla extract.

Place a generous tablespoon of the cheese in the center of each blintz. Fold in edges about a half inch and then roll up.

SHRIMP STORY

IF YOU WANT 'EM FRESH, CATCH 'EM YOURSELF

O F COURSE, LIKE MANY THINGS, IT MAKES NO SENSE, UNTIL YOU DO IT.

You get a week off. You tell your friends you're heading to Florida, the Sunshine State. They think: White wine, feelin' fine, outta reach, on the beach.

So you get there, but instead of Holiday Inn, it's some little dump of a burg. You risk tires and trim pulling your truck out onto the jagged concrete seawall. And then, by the seaweed-stinking inlet, you wait.

It gets dark. It gets cold. Fifty degrees in Florida seem like 15 in Ohio. No campfires yet. We have a better use for them than mortal comfort. You feel the first pang of a strep throat. But you stay.

And so it goes, into the night.

Wait. Boredom. No bathroom. Long about 2 a.m., the Big Dipper suddenly appears.

What a welcome sight. He's a tall Bluestone Lake West Virginian. He's got coal-miner's eyes. The crowd quietly starts unloading gear. Mr. Dipper always knows when.

Suddenly, somebody on the seawall yells: "INCOMING!" The rush is on. It's polite. But it's business.

In one hand goes the light, a Ben Raven Flame Thrower, hooked up to my truck's Delco. In the other, it's a 20-foot Stretch-Flex aluminum pole, hooked to a No. 003 Land 'Em Alive net. Between my legs is a generic bucket, with seawater.

And there they are.

Our lights play out over the narrow inlet. Incredible. Bright, shimmering diamonds carpet the water, in pairs. And best: They're swimming, toward us.

So much for land shrimping. The hapless crustaceans, for rea-

sons known only to themselves, choose a few nights in March to storm the inlet and swim the gauntlet, on their backs. When the powerful lights hit their beady eyes, they light up like sparklers, even the deep guys. You lead 'em a few feet with the net, dip and gotcha, babycakes.

Otherwise, it would take a $350,000 shrimp boat to get 'em this fresh. Fresh indeed. We've already got big pots of shrimp boil on the fires. No time to waste. This is breakfast with a big "B."

Soon, the gulls will feast on the piles of torn shrimp shells and heads, nibbling on bits of tail meat. As the sun rises and the vacationers awake to another glorious day, we pile into our vehicles, fat, happy, smelly. Time to turn in, grab some ZZZs. After all, there's no guarantee, but they may be running again, tonight.

Big Dipper once told me the only good shrimp are fresh shrimp and the only fresh

shrimp are swimming shrimp and the only swimming shrimp, hopefully, are swimming into his net.

He's right. Anything else is an approximation.

You can buy 'em frozen, peeled, precooked or "green," which means in the shell. Green is cheapest because you do the work. It's also the best, but only if you can trust your dealer.

Don't buy shrimp with black spots or ones that are limp or yellow around the edges. Don't be bashful. Take a good whiff before purchasing. Any hint of an off odor, the typical fishy smell or ammonia, and forget it. Go with the frozen.

Lots of shrimp reaching this far inland is frozen somewhere along the delivery line, and may be thawed for sale. Find this out. You don't want to re-freeze and then re-thaw them.

Shrimp are incredibly delicate things. They need their shells and should shed them only

FEATURE, MARCH 22, 1989 • In 1989, Jim Hillibish told a "shrimp story" about the value of fresh-caught crustaceans—not something readers likely thought much about as far inland as Ohio. Bish did, but he made an accommodation, and he served up a recipe in which frozen shrimp was the featured ingredient.

Garlic Shrimp with Rice

1 SMALL GREEN PEPPER, CUT IN THIN STRIPS

1 SMALL RED PEPPER, CUT IN THIN STRIPS

1/4 CUP PIGNOLI (PINE NUTS) OR SLIVERED ALMONDS

2 CLOVES GARLIC, MINCED

1 TABLESPOON MARGARINE, MELTED

1 1/3 CUPS COOKED RICE,
COOKED IN DEFATTED CHICKEN BROTH

2 TABLESPOONS FRESH PARSLEY

1 DOZEN MEDIUM SHRIMP, BOILED, BROILED OR SAUTÉED

Sauté peppers, nuts and garlic in the margarine in a large skillet over medium-high heat until tender. Add cooked rice and parsley. Stir until heated. Cook your shrimp to your liking and arrange on top, with a garnish of lemon and more parsley.

moments before cooking, if at all. Many advise to keep the shells on for most cooking techniques.

Don't believe that stuff about shrimp peeling requiring the dexterity of a neurosurgeon. Try this: Hold a green shrimp in one hand. Peel off the legs. Then peel a piece of shell from the head end. Hold this and give the tail a yank. That's it.

Larger shrimp needs deveining. With a sharp knife, slit alongside the outside curve of the shrimp. Pull out the dark vein. Thoroughly wash the shrimp in very cold water. Shrimp are so fragile, even 10 seconds of overcooking can blow it. Or, as a guest at my house recently said after a personal disaster, "It's vulcanized."

Shrimp has its own subtle flavor. When cooked in wine or a sauce, it assumes the new taste. True shrimp lovers covet them simply boiled or steamed in the shell, with a little drawn lemon butter waiting for dipping. No tartar or cocktail sauce, please. Just mounds of shrimp.

For a good shrimp boil, make a cheesecloth bag containing two cloves of garlic, two bay leaves, a whole small onion, a small peeled carrot, a cup of celery leaves, a half cup of parsley, 15 to 20 whole peppercorns or a small, dried hot pepper. Simmer this in 5 cups of lightly salted water containing a tablespoon of cider vinegar for 15 minutes. Then bring to a boil and add a pound of green shrimp, in or out of shell.

Now comes the problem: Timing. Some say turn off heat as soon as it returns to a boil. It all depends on size and freshness of your critters. I dump mine into a colander as soon as they turn pink and the steam smells like shrimp, boil or no boil. Quickly rinse with cold water. And that's it.

You can charcoal-grill fresh shrimp on shish kebab sticks. Beforehand, try marinating them in any citrus juice for 10 minutes. Then grill 2-3 minutes per side. You can sauté shrimp in butter and shallots for a minute. Add a dash of white wine and cover for another minute. But be quick.

You can broil shrimp in butter. Beware of leather. Or, you can bread it and deep fry. This to me is an ignoble, calorie-loaded end to a noble creature and to be avoided, except for the shrimp-in-a-basket joints along Route A1A in Florida.

Or, you can go to Florida, stay up all night dipping and pig out for breakfast. Heck no. I'm not telling you where. Big Dipper would peel and boil me alive.

From the simple-is-better school of shrimp cookery, try this easy but elegant dish. (Column slightly condensed.)

WHAT IT MEANS TO HAVE
TRUE 'CORDON BLEU'

WHEN YOU WATCH THE ARBY'S COMMERCIAL ON ITS CORDON BLEU SANDWICH, IMAGINE THE GAS IT CAUSES IN THE BOWELS OF THE CORDON BLEU (BLUE RIBBON) SCHOOL OF CLASSIC FRENCH CUISINE IN PARIS.

Guys, you shoulda trademarked that sucker 100 years ago.

Just about anything can be a cordon bleu these days, if it contains chicken, ham and a slice of cheese. And what a flavor combo that is, in all its versions, including Arby's.

I've seen cordon bleu braised, battered and deep fried, rolled into a dough pocket and cooked All-American style (with a can of Campbell's mushroom soup or in a toaster).

Few recipes range as widely as this one, from $65 entrées in New York French restaurants to $1 microwave popovers in our vending machines at work. I like it hot, cold, slightly warmed or, OK, whatever.

Long ago, the dish lost its capital letters, meaning it entered the generic domain. That's a shame, because the classic version is getting lost amid the noise.

People hear "French cooking" and react, "Well, I really don't have two days to prepare dinner." Not so with chicken cordon bleu. It takes but an hour, including the baking, to serve this classic French dish.

BOILING POINT, MARCH 28, 2001 • Fast food and traditional restaurants can try to duplicate the cordon bleu flavor in a sandwich, but it isn't from the Cordon Bleu school of classic French cuisine in Paris. Jim Hillibish's "Real Chicken Cordon Bleu," however, comes close to what it means to have "true" cordon bleu.

I guarantee you'll get clean plates.

An authentic bleu does require one thing that makes some people scream at the thought. It's no fair making it with boneless chicken breasts.

You need to get back in the bone-in ones. Those bones are in there for a purpose, and it's not just to prop up the chicken. They add a lot of flavor, even before cooking, and you can recycle them into chicken broth that beats anything canned or boxed.

You'll need bone-in anyway, as cordon bleu requires a larger, flatter breast than those funny little do-dads that come boned and skinned.

The word on deboning a chicken breast without removing your fingernails is "freeze." Partially freeze them for about an hour. Then the bones and skin will peel off neatly.

Another overlooked element of the original is to pound the breast between waxed paper to about half its original thickness. This does more than flatten it. It releases the membranes in the meat, creating that tenderness we all crave.

I like cordon bleu made as simply as possible, breaded and braised uncovered in a few jiggers of white wine.

A lot of recipes put the cheese on the out-side, melted at the last minute. You lose a lot of flavor if you don't bake it inside, and it seems less like, you know, a cheeseburger.

The other thing is—don't overbake it. It's

A Real Chicken Cordon Bleu

4 TABLESPOONS BUTTER
1 CUP FLOUR, SEASONED WITH SALT, PEPPER AND A TEASPOON OF DRIED TARRAGON
4 BREASTS OF CHICKEN
4 THICK SLICES AGED SWISS CHEESE, ABOUT 8 OUNCES · 4 THIN SLICES VIRGINIA-STYLE HAM
2 EGGS, LIGHTLY BEATEN · 2 CUPS BREAD CRUMBS · 1/2 CUP DRY WHITE WINE

Bone and skin chicken breasts and flatten between plastic wrap or waxed paper with a mallet, to about half of their original thickness.

Heat oven to 375 degrees. Place a slice of ham and one of cheese on each breast and roll up, securing with two or three toothpicks. Dredge each in seasoned flour and shake off excess. Coat with egg, and roll in bread crumbs.

Melt butter in a ceramic baking dish large enough to hold the chicken. Place them in the dish and coat with the butter on both sides.

Add wine. Bake for 45 minutes to an hour or until golden brown.

Baste with remaining wine-butter sauce and remove toothpicks before serving.

If you'd like a cream sauce, remove the cooked breasts and wine from the baking dish. Add a tablespoon of butter and a tablespoon of flour. Whisk to mix. Slowly add the reserved wine and 1/2 cup of cream or half and half, whisking continually until it thickens. Season with salt, white pepper and a dash of crumbled tarragon.

Serves 4 or 1 nephew.

done when a knife prick results in clear juices, and you see no pink meat.

I always make a double recipe because the breasts freeze well and can be an elegant 15-minute rerun on busy nights. I adore them sliced between two buttered pieces of French (of course) bread, with a mortar of French (of course) Dijon mustard.

Take a deep breath and try this authentic chicken cordon bleu tonight. I served it last week to my nephew. His disappeared before I finished my salad. Then he ate half of my wife's and cast longing glances at mine. I think he stopped at Arby's on the way home.

Chili North & South

Just where did this dish come from?

HERE'S YET ANOTHER REASON WHY WE SHOULD HAVE ALL BEEN COWBOYS.

I've been searching for the origins of chili. All I have is a pile of theories, although a cowboy one seems most logical to me.

I'd like to give you the original chili recipe, but it does not exist. In fact, "recipe" doesn't apply to chili. It's more an evolving state of cookery than a list of ingredients, a moving target for a six-shooter.

The Big Issue is North vs. Southwest. Chili is always red and with beans in the North. It's usually any old color but red and without beans in the Southwest. It's more of a soup in the North and more of a stew in the Southwest. After that, things get really picky.

One notion I can knock down. It looks like the chili we eat is truly American, not Mexican. Some 1600s meat stews in Mexico bore a resemblance, but I wouldn't call them chili and neither did they.

What if I told you that chili is cowboy grub borrowed from American Indians?

Some food history books indicate a staple of the early American Indians in the Southwest was a stew made of wild vegetables including garlic, peppers, onions and always meat. Sound familiar?

Later came the cowboy era in the Republic of Texas. Some of the cowboys at that time were former black slaves. Black guys often doubled as the chuck-wagon cooks.

They and their white counterparts ate an easy and tangy dish on the range that mimicked the Indian version. They called it Chlyeh, an Indian word meaning fire coals, where the dish was simmered all day. This is as close as any historic dish came to being called chili.

Note, no beans in Chlyeh. That didn't happen until the mid-1800s, when Santa Fe traders brought the dish to Cincinnati. By then, the name had been anglicized to "chili," a name also applied to the hot peppers it contains, the chile or chili.

Cincy cooks lowered the pepper head and added beans for body. They ladled in cinnamon, cloves and, eventually, tomatoes. To this day, that's the basic recipe they crave in scores of chili parlors down there.

BOILING POINT, MARCH 21, 2001 • Chili has an interesting and evolving history that has roots in both the northern and southern portions of the country. Where the chili cook hails from is crucial to how that chili will taste, Jim Hillibish assured.

Cincinnati Red Chili

2 TABLESPOONS BUTTER • 2 POUNDS LEAN GROUND BEEF

6 BAY LEAVES • 1 LARGE ONION, FINELY CHOPPED

6 GARLIC CLOVES, DICED • 1 TEASPOON CINNAMON

1/2 TEASPOON GROUND CLOVES • 4 TEASPOONS CIDER VINEGAR

1 1/2 TEASPOONS SALT • 2 TEASPOONS SWEET CHILI POWDER

1 TEASPOON GROUND CUMIN • 1/2 TEASPOON DRIED OREGANO

2 CANS (6-OUNCE) TOMATO PASTE • 16 OUNCES CANNED KIDNEY BEANS, DRAINED

Melt the butter in a heavy pot and brown the meat. Add the onions and garlic and cook until the onions are transparent (not browned). Stir in the remaining ingredients. If the flavor is too sweet, add a little more vinegar; if not spicy enough, add a little chili powder.

Bring the mixture to a boil and then lower the heat and simmer, uncovered, for 2 hours, stirring occasionally.

Cook the kidney beans in it 45 minutes before serving.

The modern-day Cincy way to eat this is over spaghetti with cheddar cheese and onion on top. Cowboys, of course, would cringe.

Serves 10 starving riverboat hands

Texas Range Chili

2 POUNDS SIRLOIN, DICED FINELY
(OR 1 POUND SIRLOIN AND 1 POUND GROUND SAUSAGE)

2 MEDIUM ONIONS, CHOPPED • 1 CUP BEER

1 CUP WATER • 1 BELL PEPPER, CHOPPED

1 JALAPEÑO PEPPER, CHOPPED • 1 GARLIC CLOVE, MINCED

2 TABLESPOONS CHILI POWDER • 1/2 TEASPOON SALT

1/4 TEASPOON CAYENNE PEPPER • 1/2 TEASPOON DRIED OREGANO

1/4 CUP CORN (MASA) FLOUR

Brown meat and onions in a heavy pot. Add beer and water, simmer 15 minutes. Add remaining ingredients except for flour and bring to a boil. Stir a small amount of hot mixture into the masa and add to chili, stirring until it thickens. Cover and simmer for 15 minutes, stirring occasionally. Add more beer if it is too thick. Adjust heat with more or less chili powder.

Feeds 6 famished range riders.

Cincinnati remains the capital of the bean-chili crowd. Texas remains the bean-free zone. The rest of us have adapted the concoction to whatever we like, and we defend it as Real Chili.

This is the secret of longevity for chili. Instead of a single recipe, it evolves every time it's made.

I'm eating what I like, and damn the history books. However, you might want to start with the two mother recipes of the chili revolution that continue to this day. These are ground zero for Southwestern cowboy and Cincinnati Northern versions.

This weekend, pick the one you like as a starting point and work in your own improvements. Bitter chocolate, venison, rattlesnake (!) and hot sauce come to mind. This way, you can claim your own chili recipe, put your name on it and maybe some day win a chili cook-off. And you can brag your brew is steeped in the pot and in history.

So here goes, two historically accurate base recipes for that dish we all love, chili.

Mom's biscuit bequest solves lifelong search

I WOULD EAT BISCUITS WITH EVERY MEAL IF I COULD FIND THE RIGHT ONES. YOU CAN THROW YOURSELF INTO THIS QUEST. THE INTERNET OFFERS 2.36 MILLION BISCUIT RECIPES FOR THE OBSESSED, LIKE ME.

I'm eating one right now—light, airy, perfectly browned, exactly what my mom would make. Then again, perhaps there are better.

Each online recipe comes with four stars and a gushing report about how these are good enough to eat right out of the oven (wrong, all need to sit a bit).

I don't actually make my favorite recipe. I watch it. I catch every rerun of Alton Brown's epic biscuit show, his most popular segment. Alton turns biscuit making into molecular physics. He got so deep into himself, his mother says his recipe is, I quote with her emphasis, "CRAZY!"

Food writers and personalities have made livings off turning simple things complex. Julia Child's biscuits include parsley and chives. Are these biscuits or salad? She takes a chance on baking powder AND baking soda plus not one but two eggs. Julia, this sounds more like pound cake.

James Beard, bless him, made his with heavy cream. Then he dipped the dough balls in melted butter. Then he took a Lipitor or two and called his doctor.

You see, there's a lot of room in a book and a lot of time in a 30-minute TV show (and 15 inches of space for this column). If you don't have anything compelling, invent it already.

Paula Deen is closer to home but no cigar. Her "authentic Southern biscuits" are little, bite-size poppers. Paula, more is much more with biscuits.

One item everybody seems to agree upon is it ain't the meat, it's the motion when it comes to biscuit making. Many cooks confuse biscuits with bread and have at it with intense kneading. Result: Cannonball biscuits.

Biscuits rise chemically with baking powder. Anything with this never needs kneading. Yeast is a different creature, alive and requiring 10 minutes of arm-wrestling.

I've discovered why all mom-made biscuits rise from the crowd of pretenders. It's not the biscuits. It's the memories of cool mornings and her cheery banter as she separated her biscuits steamy from the oven and slathered butter and honey on top. Sigh.

I've endured years of experimenting with biscuit recipes. I even did Alton's "whole nine yards." Strange thing, the answer was as close as the recipe box I inherited from my mom.

The thing to remember is to keep the rolling pin safely in the cupboard. It offers a temptation, but rolling kills tender biscuits. Mom said that's why God gave us hands, and that's the truth.

BOILING POINT, APRIL 22, 2010 • A biscuit recipe that Jim Hillibish shared in 2010 was a memory of home that was close to his heart. The "light" and "airy" biscuits were exactly what mom would have made, we know, of course, because the recipe was hers.

Jim's Mom's Biscuits

1 1/2 CUPS FLOUR, ALL PURPOSE

1/2 TEASPOON SALT

1 TABLESPOON SUGAR

1 TABLESPOON BAKING POWDER

2/3 CUP MILK, OR MORE

1/2 CUP BUTTER AT ROOM TEMPERATURE

Sift the dry ingredients into a bowl. Cut in the butter with a pastry knife or dough blender or your fingers, and mix, forming crumbles. Add milk at room temperature and stir with a wooden spoon, only until the dough forms. Add a little more milk if needed or a little more flour if excessively sticky. This depends on the flour you buy.

Dump out the dough on a lightly floured surface. Form into a circle with your hands, then press it out to a half-inch thick. Work the dough minimally. Flour a biscuit cutter and have at it.

Place dough circles on an ungreased baking sheet (Mom used a cast-iron skillet). If they touch, you will have higher, more tender biscuits. A space between them creates crispy biscuits.

Brush tops with milk and bake for 10 minutes at 425 degrees. Check for browning and bake 2 minutes more if needed.

Cool biscuits slightly on a wire rack before serving. You can reheat them in the microwave, 15 seconds on high under a damp paper towel.

Makes about 10 biscuits.

CHEESE SPAGHETTI
SAVES THE SERGEANT'S DAY

I OWE A LOT OF MY INTEREST IN COOK- ING TO ARMY MESS SGT. CHUCK HEAVER (WE CALLED HIM UP- CHUCK, BUT NOT TO HIS FACE), THE INVENTOR OF EXTRA CRUNCHY SPA- GHETTI AND SO-SLIMEY GRILLED CHEESE.

Heaver ran the mess hall, and we ran from him. If you caught his eye, he'd yell "KP, buttworm." You were dead meat, just like his meatloaf.

His mess hall was a conver- gence of dish washing and inter- national politics. If you refused to wash his dishes, he'd wash you out to Vietnam.

Heaver hated my guts more than the usual grunt guts. I had the audacity (stupidity) to sug- gest that perhaps the crunchy mouthful of his spaghetti was due to the bones ground up in his exceptionally low-grade ham- burger.

"Hellofavitch, I'm hearin' them engines on that airliner right now."

Heaver's commitment to lack of quality was easily explained. He owned a half interest in a greasy pizza carryout 15 3/4 feet from our fort's main gate. Funny thing how on crunchy spaghetti nights in the mess hall, the car- ryout was packed.

KP was unavoidable, but noth- ing in the Army regs forced any- body to eat the results. That would be against the Gene- va Convention.

This spawned creative cookery outside the mess hall. You really could bake a TV dinner on the idling radiator of a deuce and a half or toast a ham sand- wich on the smoking breach of a 155mm howitzer.

One morning, I stumbled out for KP at 4 a.m. and found Heav- er in his greasy office, greasy head in his greasy hands, almost to the point of tears amid piles of M1-A1 Army recipe cards.

"Jeeze, sarge, been eating your own food?" I said.

The Army had strict rules on food. Everybody worldwide had to at least see the same stuff on the same days. That way, they could order food by the gross megaton, and indeed it was.

Pentagon provisioning didn't take into account emergencies. Heaver that morning got an unexpected order for 1,500 hot lunches for a battalion of visit- ing ROTC cadets and barely had enough chow for his usual mess call. Plus, it was Saturday, his regular cook was off, and the ra- tions depot was closed.

"We're dead," he said.

What do you mean, "we," I thought.

"Well, I know what I'd do, cheese spaghetti."

"God, they'll transfer me to MACV," Heaver said. That was Vietnam.

"Cheese spaghetti," I said.

"That is, after I get out of the brig," he said. That was Leaven- worth.

BOILING POINT, APRIL 4, 2001 • Cheese spaghetti was dreamed up by a grouchy and grumbling mess hall cook that Jim Hillibish knew during his Army days. The sergeant had a "commitment to lack of quality," but nevertheless came up with this crunchy spaghetti dish that Jim passed on with typical Hillibish storytelling style.

"Cheese spaghetti," I said.

"And I'll lose the carryout," he moaned. That was the worst part.

"Cheese spaghetti," I said.

He looked at me like I was out of my buttworm mind. Then the light bulb came on.

"You know, maybe we could do cheese spaghetti. What the hell is that?"

"You are one brilliant son of a mother," I said, not exactly like that.

We looked through the cards, but cheese spaghetti was not on the Pentagon's list of approved foods for that day or any day. You could serve for two world wars and never see it served.

That's unfortunate because it's the easiest, cheapest and tastiest way to chow down a horde in a hurry. I learned my version in college. You could feed two frats on 5 pounds of spaghetti.

"These Rotcee meatballs aren't really Army," Heaver assumed, "so we can get away with it."

There's that word again, "we."

Anyway, I figured we had a lot of spaghetti in the pantry, as nobody on the base ate it. Ditto American cheese. I'd never seen anybody eat Heaver's grilled cheese. It kept slipping out of your hands for all the grease.

He melted bricks of cheese and butter into boiled spags all morning while I set out the Saturday breakfast that nobody ever ate.

Heaver had everything in huge pans in the ovens when he came over, wondering how long to cook it.

"I'd say it'll be done whenever they get here, but it better have a brown crust on top or you're chopped liver." He understood that.

And so it happened. The Rotcee babies filed in, hit our steam line and got huge plates of browned cheese spaghetti, salad and bread and butter. They then did something Heaver never saw in his 22 1/2 years of slapping Army chow. They came back for seconds.

I figured it was time to grasp the rapture of the moment and let him know I never again wanted to see my name on his cursed KP list, ever, not in 100 years or hell freezing over or Commies invading Ohio. Small payment for saving his behind.

"Hellofavitch, it's already done," Heaver said. No KP for you, buttworm, I'm makin' you my new cook at the carryout."

I went back to the barracks, assumed the fetal position and wanted my mommy even more than usual.

Not U.S. Army Cheese Spaghetti

1 POUND COOKED SPAGHETTI

1/4 CUP BUTTER

1/4 CUP MILK

1/2 POUND DICED Velveeta-STYLE CHEESE

1/2 POUND DICED CHEDDAR CHEESE

1 TEASPOON GARLIC POWDER

1 TEASPOON GROUND BLACK PEPPER

Heat oven to 350 degrees. Cook pasta until nearly done in a large pot of boiling water. Drain and return to pot on low heat. Immediately stir in butter until melted, followed by the remaining ingredients. Stir until creamy. Add to greased baking dish. Bake 20 minutes or until top brown.

Serves 6 civilians or 4 grunts. Easily expandable to battalion or division levels in a national emergency.

'It's rhubarb, but it really is wonderful'

I'M TRYING HARD NOT TO USE A WORD IN THIS PIECE, BUT IT WON'T WORK. SO THERE. RHUBARB. KIND OF SENDS YOUR TONGUE INTO A CRINKLE, EH? OR PERHAPS YOU'RE THINKING THIS IS ABOUT A FIGHT IN BASEBALL, ALSO CALLED A "RHUBARB."

The only fighting here comes when you try to serve it. Rhubarb, more than any other vegetable, is so universally detested, at least 75 percent of you already have stopped reading this, and the rest are food masochists.

Most folks figure we should have left rhubarb in ancient China, where they used it as a laxative. But no. Somebody imported it, and somehow it wound up in the far backyards of every home in the pre-Ex-Lax era.

Most of our rhubarb today stems (no pun) from those plants. You see, rhubarb never dies. It just keeps on producing. Talk about regular.

We had some in our backyard when we moved in. It strangely disappeared after I made but one pint of rhubarb sauce. My wife hates it. I think she had a rhubarb with the rhubarb out back, with a hoe.

So what to do with this tart (most call it biting) thing? Compost it? Until last Friday, I thought this was its best use.

I was talking about rhubarb with my neighbor. I expected Kay to flail away at it with the usual childhood tale of having to eat it "because of the starving children in China." At least those kids weren't constipated.

But no. Mention of this nasty thing launched Kay into memories of her mother's rhubarb custard pie, the only way Kay will touch the stuff.

"I know it's rhubarb, but it really is wonderful," she said.

My jaw dropped. I'd never heard rhubarb described in so friendly terms. We are talking about rhubarb, aren't we?

I thought maybe I could get a taste of this miracle and left a few dozen hints for a slice of the next pie. Next day, a whole pie arrived, delivered by Kay and our block's most famous golden retriever, the rhubarb-hating Sadie Mae.

I had a berry pie last summer made by Kay's mom, Milly Carper. It was the best, until the rhubarb one arrived. That one ranks right up there with my own mom's fresh peach pie, perhaps better because it is such a surprise.

Milly should be on all the talk shows promoting rhubarb. Her pie had no hint of the cardboard-glue taste we associate with the stuff. It had none of the stringy fiber that

BOILING POINT, MAY 2, 2001 • Friends, family and neighbors often supplied Jim Hillibish with fodder for his recipe file. One recipe that came to light—and saved the reputation of much rhubarb—was Milly Carper's Rhubarb Pie.

Milly Carper's Rhubarb Custard Pie

3 EGGS, BEATEN SLIGHTLY

ADD 2 2/3 TABLESPOONS OF MILK

STIR IN:

2 CUPS SUGAR

4 TABLESPOONS FLOUR

1/2 TEASPOON NUTMEG

4 CUPS CUT-UP RHUBARB (INCH PIECES)

Dot the filling with 1 tablespoon butter. Pour it into a 9-inch pastry-lined baking plate. Cover with a lattice dough top. Bake in a 400-degree oven for 20 minutes, reducing it to 375 degrees for 30 to 40 minutes more, until nicely browned. Cool before slicing.

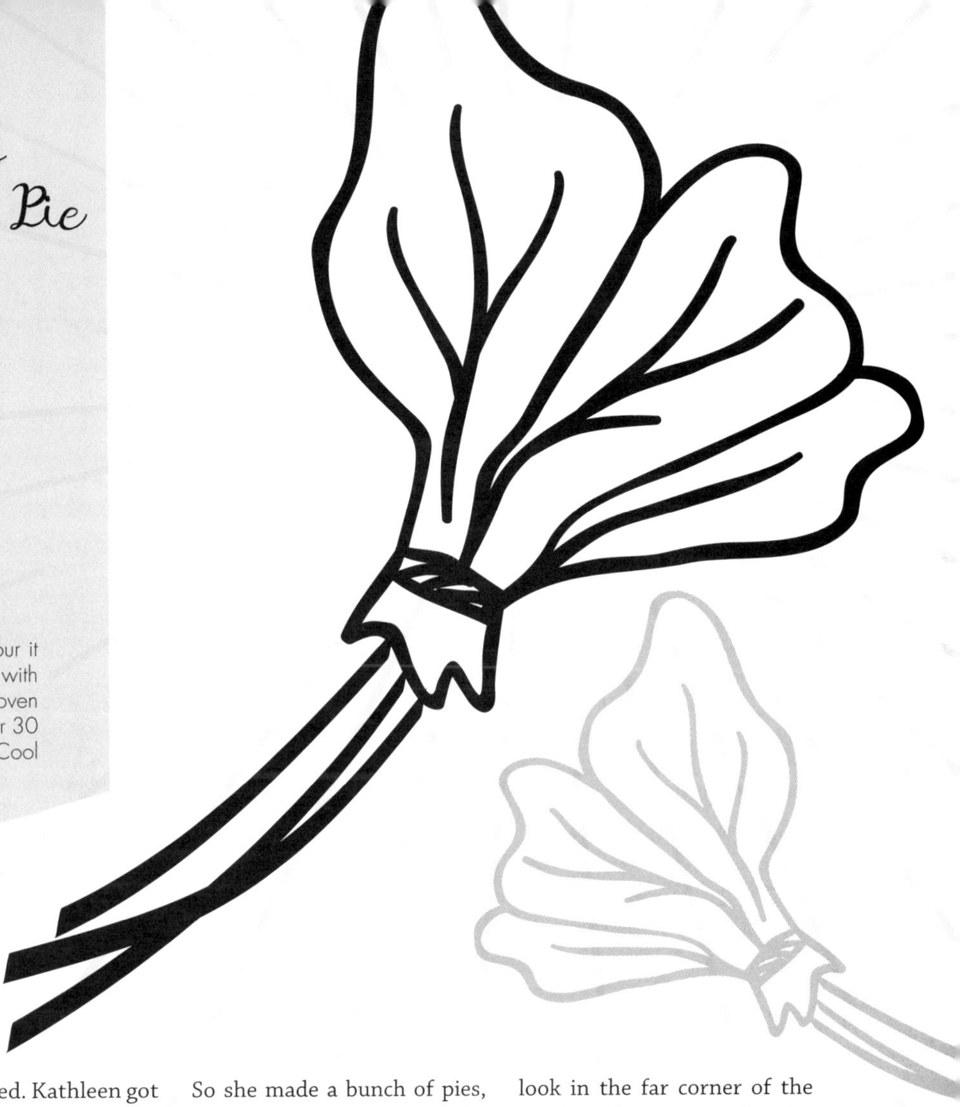

sticks in the teeth and gags in the throat.

I cut a piece for my rhubarb-detracting wife.

"Well, it's not my all-time favorite pie," she said, "but it's better than any you've ever baked. Translation: four and a half stars out of five.

Two days later, and the pie had disappeared. Kathleen got the last slice. We ate more rhubarb during the weekend than we had for the past 25 years.

Milly isn't one to take rhubarb critics at their word. A few years ago, she heard that none of the kids at her grandsons' school, Mason Elementary, ever had tasted rhubarb. So she made a bunch of pies, and all pigged out. Even the teachers loved them. That perhaps is the world's most compelling reason to try rhubarb pie. If modern kids will love it ...

So forget all your bad memories of 'barb and bake this pie. Rush to your store and look in the far corner of the produce department for the rhubarb pile. Buy only crisp stems and fresh leaves. Memorize the price, as the checkout clerk won't know what the heck it is.

And, as Milly says, "Enjoy." No rhubarb over rhubarb, nevermore.

THERE'S ONLY ONE WAY TO GET AUTHENTIC MASHED POTATOES

W E OFTEN WIND UP AT MOUNTAIN JACK'S IN PROM SEASON, YOU KNOW, WHEN THE HIGH SCHOOLERS ARRIVE IN GOWNS WORTH MORE THAN THE BLUE BOOK VALUE OF OUR CAR OUT IN THE LOT.

I've studied MJ's and figured out why they were successful. It's not the prime rib, which is great, or the veggie sides, which are average. It's the most simple thing on the menu, the mashed potatoes.

Build a good mashed potato, and they will come, with their credit cards.

The trouble with mashed pots at most local restaurants is they have no idea what we want in them. You could go to KFC and get Southern style, called "creamed potatoes." Out West, they call them "whipped" potatoes, and it's the same result. We call it pota- to soup.

Or you could try an expensive joint and get no potato options whatsoever.

"Mashed potatoes are too, you know, homely," a snob waiter told me.

Or you could simply stay home and do your own with a little inspiration.

Like Mountain Jack's, I like my potatoes to be potatoes. Leave the vichyssoise to the French. I like a good potato flavor and a chunky (they call it "smashed") texture. Potatoes with tooth. That's the picture.

That old hand power mixer is the death of mashed potatoes. It destroys everything, especially the texture. If I want velvet, I'll eat chocolate.

To get back to your grandma's recipe, you need a real potato masher (not the German hand grenade). This is a heavy metal plate with holes in it attached to a stout handle. It smashes your boilers, but does not cream

them like a mixer. That's a big difference.

Some of the later ones have a squiggly wire masher and a painted wood handle.

You may have to go to an antique store to find a masher. It's worth the search and will cost around $10. (You can use it to smash berries to make jam in the summer.)

I like red potatoes for mashing. The Idaho bakers are too grainy for me. Pontiac reds or Yukon Golds are ideal.

I've noticed most folks add too much milk to their mashed potatoes. The milk should go in by the dribble. It's dangerous following a recipe that dictates a specific amount of liquid. How much you use depends on your taste and the kind of potatoes you're using. Dribble. Taste. Dribble. That's it.

You want the potatoes to be solid enough to hold a well of gravy. Too much milk gives you a glop that swims around the plate.

Part of that glop comes from adding too much butter. Mashed potatoes need a little mixed in the pot, but the major buttering

---

BOILING POINT, MAY 15, 2002 • Mashed potatoes, smashed potatoes, creamed potatoes or whipped potatoes. No matter what you call this creamy potato side dish, we probably all can agree that such potatoes, though secondary to the entrée, can make or break a meat meal.

Jim's Garlic Mashed Potatoes

6 MEDIUM POTATOES, PEELED AND LARGE CUBED

2 QUARTS BOILING WATER

THREE CLOVES GARLIC, PEELED AND DICED

1 TEASPOON SALT

MILK • BUTTER

Boil the potatoes with the garlic in salted water, until fork tender. Drain and return to hot pan. Mash for a minute or so with a potato masher. Dribble in the milk, stirring, until the potatoes reach the texture you desire. Serve with butter, salt and pepper at the table and snipped chives or parsley for a garnish.

Serves 3 to 4 but double the recipe for leftovers.

Potato Pancakes

3 CUPS LEFTOVER MASHED POTATOES

1 LARGE EGG • 1/4 CUP FLOUR

1/4 CUP BUTTER OR OIL (OR COMBINED)

Stir the egg and flour into the potatoes, mixing until it forms a sticky, dough-like consistency. You may need to add more flour depending on your potatoes. You could add finely diced onions or chives for a different flavor.

Heat the oil or butter in a heavy skillet. Roll out the dough to half-inch thickness on a floured board. Flour the top of a 3-inch diameter glass proof plastic container. Use it to cut your pancakes.

Fry them until golden brown on one side, then turn.

Serve hot. Some folks like applesauce or sour cream on the top or side. For cheese pancakes, add a 1/2 cup of grated Monterey Jack or Swiss cheese while mixing the dough.

Serves 3.

Potato Soup

3 CUPS LEFTOVER MASHED POTATOES

1 CUP VEGETABLE OR CHICKEN STOCK

1 CUP SLICED LEEKS OR ONIONS • 1 GARLIC CLOVE, FINELY MINCED

SNIPPED CHIVES • SALT AND WHITE PEPPER TO TASTE

Thinly slice the leeks and cook with garlic for 15 minutes in the broth, or until tender. Put the potatoes in a blender and pour in the broth and leeks. Blend until smooth. This may be served warm or chilled, garnished with chives or parsley. If serving cold, chill the bowls in the freezer.

Serves 3 to 4.

should come at the table, by the eaters. It, and the salt, are preferential things.

I've found garlic and potatoes are a cozy marriage. You can make a friendly garlic mashed by adding cloves of minced garlic to the potato boiling water. This offers just a hint of garlic, nothing hot or overpowering.

I also like snipped chives added just before serving.

The big rule is to always make more than you need. Leftovers are great, diluted with stock as a soup or formed into potato pancakes, all nice and crusty.

P.S... A friend of mine (he edits this column) says olive oil is a good, low-cholesterol substitute for butter when you do the mashing. He likes buttermilk in his, saying, "You don't even need gravy." Sounds like a keeper.

Macaroni & Cheese
BEYOND THE BOX

YOU KNOW THE DRILL. DRAG YOUR BONES HOME AFTER A 10-HOUR DAY AT WORK, ONLY TO FACE THE ONSLAUGHT OF A FAMISHED FAMILY.

So you reach for Old Reliable in the pantry, the one thing they never refuse: Kraft macaroni and cheese. Fifteen minutes later, it's suppertime.

I still eat this stuff. It got me through college and the Army (at 12 cents a box), and it's certainly a reliable old friend.

Still, when food is this easy, we forget we can take it up a notch. If you like 15-minute manufactured mac and cheese, you'll crave the 35-minute from-scratch version.

This is the mac and cheese the Italian ladies baked at your grade school in the 1950s on no-meat Fridays. I can almost taste it at Frazer School, huge piles of it, all you can eat for a quarter, with brown crust on top. Totally legendary. Oh my, I want some now.

There's nothing complicated here. It makes the cheese sauce in the pan. I added bread crumbs on top because I like the crunch. Another notch up: Use leftover garlic bread.

Unlike the stove-top variety, this one must be baked. It changes the texture of the pasta and drives that cheese flavor into it. Baking is worth the effort here.

Consider this a basic recipe, excellent as it is, but ready to do your bidding. I really like drained canned tuna in here, combining the two mangas of my childhood. You could add some tomatoes for a change, and some ham. Or try diced chili peppers. That's different.

Cheddar's good, but not the best melting cheese. I like variations such as Velveeta or Monterey jack. A white cheese combined with a half cup of Parmesan is nice. Some folks even use, ahem, Cheez Whiz.

A welcome change is a scoop of your best chili atop each serving, the ultimate use of leftover red. There's nothing like the taste of chili and mac and cheese on the same fork.

What about bacon and shredded chicken breast, with salsa and crumbled tortilla chips instead of bread crumbs on top? Max mex mac. Ballistic.

BOILING POINT, MAY 9, 2001 • Macaroni and cheese is quick and easy and tasty, that's why it's a favorite of moms who are trying to feed families after working to raise money to meet their household food budget. Maybe that's why Jim Hillibish called this recipe "The Mother Of All Macaroni And Cheese."

Our school mac always came with jumbo elbow macaroni. I keep looking for them in the stores but cannot find any. These were the big guys, chewy and more than an inch long.

To be true to your school (cafeteria), you must bake the mac in big aluminum sheet pans. This is one of those dishes that tastes better made in a large quantity. Not to worry. It freezes well, but it will need a little refresher of milk while reheating.

This beautiful dish is ready to eat when the top browns and the sauce is bubbling all around and spilling onto your oven floor. Remember to put a cookie sheet under the baking pan.

Enough of the words. Rush to your kitchen and dive in.

The Mother Of All Macaroni & Cheese

2 CUPS UNCOOKED ELBOW MACARONI

2 CUPS GRATED MILD CHEDDAR CHEESE

1/4 CUP BUTTER

2 LARGE EGGS

1 1/2 CUPS MILK

2 HEELS OF DAY-OLD ITALIAN BREAD, BUTTERED AND FINELY DICED

SALT AND FRESHLY GROUND PEPPER

GRATED ONION (OPTIONAL, TO TASTE)

PAPRIKA (OPTIONAL)

Boil macaroni three-quarters the length of your usual time. Drain and dump into a buttered baking dish. Mix in butter in small pieces, most of the cheese, and salt, pepper and onion.

Spread bread crumbs on top. Beat eggs and milk together and pour over the bread crumbs. Sprinkle on remaining cheese and top with paprika. Bake at 375 degrees for at least 30 minutes or until top browns and sauce bubbles.

NOTE: If you want to add extras such as ham, tuna or whatever, stir in before adding the bread crumbs.

Serves 4 adults or 2 Frazer School fourth graders.

ENJOYING STEAK ON A BURGER BUDGET

WITH FOOD PRICES ON THE INCREASE, YOU'LL PROBABLY BE READING COOKING STORIES ABOUT DOING A LOT WITH A LITTLE. LET ME BE THE FIRST TO JOIN THE FRAY.

Bottom round steak is as low as you can get with beef, on the animal and on the price sticker. Last week, I converted $1.43 worth into a surprising repast for two, worthy of company.

You instantly think "tough" at $2.29 a pound, and you're right. I chose two time-honed techniques to tenderize it: marinating and whaling away with a meat hammer.

Then I added a third one, the beef-taming Swiss steak trick where you pound seasoned flour into the meat and then slowly braise it.

Result: No knives necessary, and a wonderful steak flavor, best-ever bottom round from my kitchen.

Three hours ahead, I made a marinade of soy sauce, dashes of Worcestershire sauce and balsamic vinegar, garlic and black pepper. I bagged it and the beef.

Soy is famous for relaxing tough tendons of meat. It did its deed.

Then I seasoned some flour with pepper and pounded it into both sides of the beef. I felt the shoe leather evaporate under my hammer.

A fast sauté in olive oil with onions and mushrooms browned it nicely. Then I added the marinade and water, covered it and slow cooked it for 90 minutes on the stove top.

BOILING POINT, MAY 5, 2004 • Even in the worst of economic times, a good steak is a special meal that most meat eaters relish. So, Jim Hillibish told his readers how to make a more inexpensive cut of meat more tender and palatable.

Result: Mouthwatering aroma throughout the house, totally tender steak of excellent flavor, worthy of wolfing. A buck forty-three never tasted this good.

I splurged a bit and boiled four ears of our first sweet corn of the season. I boiled some potatoes and dressed them with fresh parsley sautéed in melted butter.

In all, the meal cost less than four bucks or a trip to the sandwich shop, for one of us.

Fuel prices, plus the improving economy, are behind the food price rise. I guess it had to happen. We've been getting away with food steals for years. We still have the cheapest groceries in the world, as a percentage of our earnings, if that's any consolation.

Eating on the cheap doesn't mean eating with lowered expectations. Cheap indeed can be the mother of invention.

Jim's Cheapsteak

ABOUT 2/3 OF A POUND OF BEEF BOTTOM ROUND STEAK

1/4 CUP SOY SAUCE

1 TEASPOON BALSAMIC VINEGAR

DASH WORCESTERSHIRE SAUCE

2 CLOVES OF GARLIC, MINCED

DASH OF FRESHLY GROUND BLACK PEPPER

1/4 CUP FLOUR

1/2 CUP ONIONS, DICED

1/4 CUP MUSHROOMS, SLICED

1 TEASPOON OLIVE OIL

1 CUP WATER

Prepare the marinade of soy sauce, vinegar, Worcestershire, garlic and pepper in a plastic food bag. Marinate the beef at least 2 hours. Then spread the flour on a cutting board and season with pepper. Rub it into both sides of the steak.

Pound both sides with a meat-tenderizing hammer. You're finished when the flour is pressed into the meat and almost disappears.

Heat oil in a large frying pan. Add steak and sear both sides, about 3 minutes each. Add onions and mushrooms. Pour in the marinade and enough water to almost cover. Cover with a tight-fitting lid and slowly simmer for 60 to 90 minutes or until fork tender. Check every 15 minutes and add more water if needed.

Serve smothered in the gravy with the onions and mushrooms on top.

Serves 2 on a hamburger budget.

FOR PERFECT HOME-BAKED BREAD,
NO NEED TO KNEAD

"**WITHOUT BREAD, EVERY-BODY'S AN ORPHAN.**"

This Italian observation is centuries old. James Beard takes a modern stab at it: "Bread is the most fundamentally satisfying of all foods."

That is, if you bake your own.

Perfect bread is a constant quest. Recipes for decades have expanded faster than yeast rises. Perhaps it has something to do with authors paid by the word. Some cookbooks are up to 20 pages on how to bake white bread. For nonreaders, The Food Network offers 60-minute tutorials.

If bread-making recipes confound you with their exact kneading dictums and chemist-like formulary, take a deep breath and don't give up.

Or start with the right recipe.

Many home bakers approach their craft as a challenge. The goal is to replicate those wonderful $7 loaves of artisanal bread in the bakery. In most cases, that's futile. Pro bakers have special bread ovens. These control heat and humidity exactly for perfect loaves. They use steam jets, found in no consumer oven.

Perfectly Simple and Good

Bread is 6,000 years old. It was one of the first prepared foods. The basic recipe for white bread is simple and fundamentally unchanged:

2 1/2 CUPS WARM WATER • 2 TEASPOONS ACTIVE DRY YEAST

8 CUPS ALL-PURPOSE FLOUR • 1 TABLESPOON SALT

Proof yeast in water, then mix remaining ingredients into it. Allow dough to rise for an hour. Punch down and place in baking tins. Allow to double in bulk. Bake 40 minutes in a 375-degree oven.

False Starts

Inventors keep trying to create a device to speed bread-making. KitchenAid in 1908 rolled out the first electric mixer. It soon added a dough hook for bread work. Using a mixer saves time and muscle power, but be careful not to overknead the dough.

Plastic bread-kneading knives arrived with food processors in 1973. Their friction heats the dough, toughening it. Dough easily becomes overkneaded here, producing fine-grain loaves with no character.

Panasonic in 1986 introduced a bread machine. You poured in the ingredients, and it did the rest. This was a hit appliance for about five years. Then came the realization that beyond the tech glitz, machine bread was closer to Wonder Bread than gourmet.

FINALLY, A NEW RECIPE

Bread has endured its fads. The latest is no-knead recipes baked in a Dutch oven, via The New York Times, no less.

The Times' recipe, adapted from Sullivan Street Bakery, sets a record for bread brevity.

FEATURE, JUNE 24, 2010 • Is kneading bread before baking too much work for you, so tiresome to the fingers that it makes you run out to buy a bagged loaf? Bish found a "perfect" home-baked bread with no kneading necessary in the recipe.

No-Knead Bread

1/4 TEASPOON DRY YEAST

1 5/8 CUPS WARM WATER

3 CUPS FLOUR

1 1/4 TEASPOONS SALT

Mix this and allow to rise 8 hours at room temperature. It's ready when the surface is bubbly. Pour out the dough on a floured board (it will be sticky). Dust with flour and place in an oiled Dutch oven. Allow to rise until it doubles.

Cover and bake 30 minutes at 450 degrees. Remove the lid and bake another 15 to 20 minutes until the loaf is golden.

The original recipe is at www.nytimes.com.

Bread Baking Glossary

ALL-PURPOSE FLOUR: A combination of hard and soft wheat flours with a medium amount of gluten suitable for bread baking.

BAGUETTE: A long, thin classic French loaf, crusty on outside, soft on inside.

BATTER BREAD: Yeast bread that is stirred, not hand-kneaded. The thick, pourable batter produces a coarser texture than kneaded.

BLOOM: The way bread opens up during baking after it has been scored with a knife. Bloomed bread is more crusty.

BREAD BRICK: Also a pizza stone, a ceramic baking surface approximating a brick oven. Heat the brick and coat with cornmeal. Slide dough on the brick and bake.

CARBON DIOXIDE: A byproduct of yeast fermentation that rises the bread. Kneading helps to evenly divide it in a loaf.

COOLRISE: Dough that slowly rises overnight in a refrigerator, allowing flavor to form.

CRUMB: The interior texture, tenderness and general feel of bread. Kneaded breads are fine crumb. Batter breads are coarser.

FLAT TOP: The dome of the loaf does not hold up and flattens during baking, usually caused by too much yeast (over proofing), too little flour or excess rising time. Also called a wrinkler.

SPONGE: Liquid and yeast, mixed with a little flour and allowed to rise for about 30 minutes. Note that salt is added after the period. This results in lighter bread with an airy crumb.

PROOF: A test for active yeast. Place yeast in warm water with a dash of sugar. It should be bubbly and double in volume in about 15 minutes.

SALT: Serves as a flavor enhancer and improves the ability of gluten to form a fine-textured crumb.

THWACK: The hollow sound when a baked loaf is thumped, indicating it is done.

YEAST: A single-cell organism that ferments the carbohydrates in bread, producing alcohol and sugar.

BEST BREAD BOOK BETS

"BEARD ON BREAD," by James Beard (1973, Knopf, $12): Many consider this the bible of bread-making. The hardcover is out of print, but available used. A paperback is the reprint.

"THE PANERA BREAD COOK-BOOK," by Panera Bread Team (2004, Clarkson Potter, $18.95): Many, but not all, of the bread-baking secrets of this highly successful enterprise.

"THE BREAD AND BUTTER BOOK," by Diana Sutton (2008, Good Life Press): A fundamental book with creative, from-scratch recipes.

"THE BREAD BAKER'S APPRENTICE," by Peter Reinhart (2001, Ten-Speed Press, $35): A how-to book looking over the shoulders of French bread chefs.

FREEZER JAM
SAVES SWEAT ON HOT SUMMER DAYS

WOULD THAT WE COULD DO OUR CANNING IN THE COLD OF JANUARY.

But no. We always pick the hottest days of the summer to stand around a boiling stove. Oh, well.

One of the many surprises you'll find when shopping for an old house is an ancient stove, in the basement. No, this is not some sort of Y2K paranoia, or perhaps Y1K. That stove, in the summer coolness of the cellar, is the canning stove.

I usually can in the semi-nude, but that's not a great idea when a jar explodes. I find myself rushing outside for a breath of fresh air. Ninety degrees seems cool when it's 120 in your kitchen.

So imagine my shock when Ida Miller's "no cook" jam recipes arrived. Messages from heaven.

We set a record for our strawberry crop this year. I was picking half-gallons worth per day for three weeks. With strawberries out the wazoo, making jam can take eons the old-style way of boiling this, boiling that, boil the jars, boil the lids, boil your brains.

That heat is critical in canning. It destroys the bacteria that could turn Ma's berry jelly into a chemical warfare agent. So I get a little suspicious about no-cook anything.

Not to worry here. These no-cook jam recipes have a second name, "freezer jam." You can refrigerate them for up to three weeks, or freeze them in plastic containers for months. Cooling here takes the place of the searing heat of the boiled jams.

Just make sure all of your canning gear, including the containers, is spotless, and you should have no problems. And don't forget allowing the stuff to sit in the containers at room temperature for 24 hours. Otherwise, you'll be making syrup instead of jam.

The flavor and texture of these are different than the heated variety. Freezer jam to me is fresher and "looser." It's a pleasant change, but, of course, I still like my boiled jams.

So, park your canning kettle and put some clothes on (you'll be opening the fridge a lot). I use liquid pectin to avoid even cooking that.

Try some of these and save some energy, too. They are easy and good consumers of bumper crops. For those of you who adore store-bought jam, we've included a no-cook barbecue sauce that's good on chicken and ribs but terrible on buttered muffins. OK, so I got the jars mixed up.

FEATURE, JUNE 27, 2001 • No matter how much you might like to do all your canning in the winter, to heat the kitchen in cold months, we do it in summer, when the weather warms and the fruits and vegetables take to the vines. Jim found a warm-weather twist to food preservation: make freezer jam.

No-Cook Blueberry Jam

3 CUPS CRUSHED BLUEBERRIES, FRESH OR FROZEN

5 CUPS SUGAR • 2 TABLESPOONS LEMON JUICE

2 PACKS LIQUID PECTIN, SUCH AS CERTO

Measure prepared berries into a large bowl. Add sugar and mix well. Let stand for 10 minutes. Stir in liquid fruit pectin and lemon juice. Continue to stir for 3 minutes until most of the sugar is dissolved. Pour into clean canning jars or plastic containers and cover tightly with lids. Let stand at room temperature until set, up to 24 hours. Store in freezer or up to 3 weeks in refrigerator.

No-Cook Peachberry Jam

1 CUP CRUSHED RASPBERRIES • 1 CUP PEELED, FINELY CHOPPED PEACHES

3 1/4 CUP SUGAR • 2 TABLESPOONS LEMON JUICE

1 PACK LIQUID FRUIT PECTIN

Measure prepared fruits into a large bowl. Add sugar and mix well. Let stand for 10 minutes. Stir in lemon juice and liquid fruit pectin. Continue to stir for 3 minutes until most of the sugar is dissolved. Pour into clean canning jars or plastic containers. Cover with tight lids and let stand at room temperature until set (may take 24 hours). Store in freezer, or for 3 weeks in refrigerator.

No-Cook Barbecue Sauce

1/4 CUP BROWN SUGAR, FIRMLY PACKED • 1 TABLESPOON BALSAMIC VINEGAR

1 TABLESPOON WATER • 1 TABLESPOON MINCED ONION

1 TEASPOON MINCED GARLIC • 2 TABLESPOONS WORCESTERSHIRE SAUCE

2 TABLESPOONS DIJON MUSTARD • FRESHLY GROUND PEPPER

Mix all ingredients, Store in refrigerator or freezer until ready to use. Stir before using.
Makes about 1/2 cup.

No-Cook Strawberry Jam

2 TABLESPOONS LEMON JUICE

1 PACK LIQUID FRUIT PECTIN

4 CUPS SUGAR

1 3/4 CUPS MASHED STRAWBERRIES

Combine lemon juice and pectin; mix well in small bowl. In large bowl, combine sugar and berries; let sit 10 minutes. Add small bowl contents to large bowl and stir for 3 minutes. Fill canning jars or containers 1/2 inch from top, wipe clean, cover at once with tight lid. Let stand 24 hours at room temperature before freezing.

TALKING TUNA

It's time this fish gained the respect it deserves

WE HAVE ONE OF THOSE OLD HOUSES WITH A FLOOR-TO-CEILING PANTRY JUST OFF THE KITCHEN. OF COURSE, IT LOOKS LIKE A GROCERY STORE. AMAZING HOW YOUR BELONGINGS ALWAYS FILL YOUR STORAGE SPACE.

More than one person has asked to see our larder and always exclaims, "Twelve cans of tuna." A main course for two that costs 45 cents seems so anti-Martha Stewart.

Many of you are biased against this underappreciated seafood. You're prejudiced by the Saturday-night tuna casseroles your mothers made to save money and do a meal in a minute.

Can canned tuna be more than canned tuna? Would you serve it to your boss? The surprising answer is yes, and yes.

You must look beyond American recipes to find great tuna dishes. Americans are stuck in tuna poverty. Many of us consumed canned tuna in the short-cash days when the college and Army mess-hall fare (there was no difference) was inedible.

If you can push yourself off this mindset, you'll find tuna worthy of candles and your finest plastic china.

In Europe, canned tuna is a delicacy costing many times what we pay. A friend of ours from England was amazed at the price here. He took home a case. (I've tried the more expensive imported tuna, and frankly, Charlie's easily the equal.)

Tuna is my kitchen 911. When all else fails, and my wife is coming home in 20 minutes, I reach for a flat can. She never complains.

Would you order canned tuna in a restaurant? Like fun. But if you order the antipasto appetizer in many a fine Italian eatery, you'll find tuna in there with the imported olives and expensive cheeses and artichoke hearts. So there.

The secret of great tuna dishes is the extra ingredients. I know, it sounds perfectly insane to mix it with $45 cognac or $10 olive oil or $12 French cheese, but it works.

I took a clue and added flaked tuna to my marinated pasta salad. Good move. I ran out of pepperoni one night when we craved homemade pizza. Tuna made it better.

The stuff instantly turns a summer salad into a real meal. Chill some with your favorite salsa and chopped, hard-boiled eggs. Spoon over Romaine and bib lettuce with just-picked tomatoes. This is more than good. Tuna canners have attempted to remake their product by using spring water instead of oil. I still like the oil, despite the calorie boost. The watered version loses flavor.

Please, let canned tuna be canned tuna. The new aseptic tuna pouches, while boosting the price, fail to impress me. They almost taste too, I don't know, is the word fresh?

If you travel to Spain, you'll find tuna in those wonderful tapas appetizers they sell for $6.50 each, and the cans (are) in the Dumpster out back. In France, tuna graces platters of fine cheese, bread and grapes. The Chinese and Japanese are so jealous of their tuna fishing grounds, they've gone to war over them.

So there. Point made, but you need proof. Pop a can and try these extravagant recipes. I have a notion you'll never again make fun of tuna.

FEATURE, JUNE 20, 2001 • Tuna tetrazzini, tuna nicoise, terrace tuna pie—even the names sound a little more sophisticated than their main ingredient, "canned tuna in oil." That's because Jim Hillibish believed that tuna, even the lowly canned kind, deserved a little respect.

Tuna Nicoise

FROM FRANCE

Est-il un topper de salade d'ete, ou un sandwich?
(It's a summer salad topper, or a sandwich?)

2 CANS TUNA PACKED IN OIL (6 1/2 OUNCES EACH)

1 SWEET RED PEPPER, ROASTED, PEELED,
CORED, SEEDED AND JULIENNED

1 SWEET YELLOW PEPPER, PREPARED SAME AS RED

1 PICKLED JALAPEÑO PEPPER, SEEDED AND MINCED

1/4 CUP DICED RED ONION

2 TABLESPOONS CHOPPED, PITTED CALAMATA OLIVES

2 TABLESPOONS CAPERS · 1 BUNCH WATERCRESS, TRIMMED

Vinaigrette Dressing

EXTRA VIRGIN OLIVE OIL

2 TEASPOONS FRESH OREGANO LEAVES, CHOPPED

1/4 TEASPOON SALT

1/4 TEASPOON FRESHLY GROUND BLACK PEPPER

3 TABLESPOONS RED-WINE VINEGAR

1 CLOVE GARLIC, MINCED

1 TEASPOON DIJON MUSTARD

Roast peppers by holding over heat with tongs until skin blackens. Place in paper bag, close and allow to cool. Peel off skin.

Dressing: Drain oil from tuna into glass measuring cup. Add olive oil to make 1/3 cup. Place oil in blender with remaining vinaigrette ingredients and blend.

In bowl, mix vegetables, olives and capers. Remove some of the soft inside from a loaf of French bread, cut in half lengthwise. Brush inside loaf with some dressing; add remainder to vegetable mixture. Mix in tuna gently, leaving chunks.

Grill bread, oiled side down, until toasted. Mound tuna mixture into toasted sides. Top with watercress and close. Slice into 4-inch wide sandwiches.

Serves 2 to 4.

Terrace Tuna Pie

FROM ENGLAND

"I'd just as soona eat me some tuna."
Edgerton Reimes IV

1 9-INCH UNBAKED PASTRY SHELL · 2 TABLESPOONS BUTTER

1/2 CUP CELERY, DICED · 1 CUP SLICED ONION RINGS

1 CUP CANNED TUNA · 1 1/2 CUPS WHITE CHEESE, SHREDDED

3 EGGS · 1/2 TEASPOON PEPPER

PINCH RED PEPPER FLAKES · 1 TEASPOON SALT

2/3 CUP HALF AND HALF

Sauté the onion rings and celery in butter until the onion is soft and golden. Spoon alternate layers of tuna, cheese (your choice—use sharp or Swiss), and the onion-celery mix into pie shell. In bowl, beat together eggs, cream, salt and pepper. Pour into pastry shell over other ingredients. Bake 400 degrees until firm, about 30 to 40 minutes. When knife point inserted into center comes out clean, filling is set. May be decorated with tomato wedges or cherry tomatoes. Cool slightly before cutting.

Serves 6 Brits or 4 Americans.

Aperitivo

FROM SPAIN

El atun de la lata sea tan bueno como caviar?
(Can tuna be as good as caviar?)

18-OUNCE CAN OF PITTED BLACK OLIVES, CHOPPED

4 OUNCES CAPERS · 2 OUNCES ANCHOVY FILLETS (OPTIONAL)

2 OUNCES CANNED TUNA IN OIL · SHOT GLASS OF COGNAC

Crush ingredients with the round handle end of a utensil. Add cognac. Chill, covered, for 2 hours. Place in a glass bowl resting in crushed ice. Serve as spread with crusty fresh bread chunks.

Serves 8.

Tuna Tetrazzini

FROM ITALY

Cazuela del atun de no su madre
(Not your mother's tuna casserole)

8 OUNCES THIN SPAGHETTI,
CUT 2 INCHES LONG

1/4 CUP BUTTER · 1/4 CUP FLOUR

SALT · 1 TEASPOON NUTMEG
(FRESHLY GROUND IS BEST)

2 CUPS CHICKEN BROTH

1 CUP LIGHT CREAM OR HALF AND HALF

1/4 CUP MARSALA WINE (OPTIONAL)

1/4 CUP PARMESAN CHEESE, FRESHLY GRATED

2 CANS (6 1/2 OUNCES EACH) TUNA,
DRAINED AND FLAKED

1/4 CUP SWEET RED PEPPER, DICED

1/2 POUND FRESH MUSHROOMS, SLICED

1 EGG YOLK · 1/2 CUP FRESH PARSLEY, CHOPPED

Cook spaghetti al dente, drain and place into buttered bowl. Melt butter over low heat, blend in flour, salt and nutmeg, and stir constantly until mixture is smooth.

Remove from heat, whisk in broth and cream, put back on heat, and bring to a boil, whisking constantly until thickened. Stir in wine and cheese.

Add sauce to spaghetti. Add tuna, pepper, mushrooms and egg yolk to spaghetti mixture, and toss. Pour into buttered baking dish and bake uncovered at 350 degrees for 30 minutes. Sprinkle parsley over top just before serving.

Serves 8.

THE FLAVOR SECRET IS OUT—
IT'S CILANTRO

So you're eating some enchiladas and wondering, "What IS that taste?"

Then you're having some Chinese chicken with "fragrant green" and wondering, "Huh?"

I like an occasional English gin and tonic, and yep, there's that taste again.

I could go on. Why not? You'll find the taste in some chewing gum, some Passover dishes and, yes, even in a few hot dogs and imported cigarettes.

So weird. All from one herb, the only one related to a carrot, by the way. There's not even agreement on what to call this puppy. Names range from Chinese parsley to coriander to cilantro.

If this isn't compelling enough, rush to your store for a bunch of cilantro and create your own "fragrant green" cuisine.

If you like history on a plate, this one's a museum piece. Cilantro has been cultivated for thousands of years and eons of cultures. It took that long to reach our local grocery stores.

I'm thanking the Latin Americans for this gift. As their numbers increase here, we're seeing more of their fresh condiments in our stores. With fresh cilantro, Mexican and Spanish cuisines are just the beginning.

Hereabouts, we call the leaves cilantro (Spanish) and the seeds coriander (Greek). That dual personality indicates the range of this herb.

Nobody agrees on what cilantro tastes like, probably because it's an original flavor. People who eat it often use "fresh tasting" to describe it. That's good enough for most of us. Cilantro adds a fresh breeze to everything it touches.

Be sure to get the fresh. The freeze-dried stuff is useless.

Cilantro looks like parsley, but don't use it like parsley. The latter has a somewhat neutral taste when cooked. There's nothing generic or flimsy about cilantro.

I don't have enough room to list all the things cilantro can flavor, breakfast to supper. Before you plunge in, try a little first. Not everybody likes the taste (some say it's "soapy"). Others insist it does everything from improving your sex life to easing the pains of birthing.

If that's not enough to get you moving, consider the joys of growing your own. The round seeds produce a nice patch of self-seeding plants that ward off bugs and rabbits. They release that fresh aroma as you brush by the leaves.

Fresh-picked is flavor at 100 mph. The fresher it is, the less you'll need. I make a cilantro chicken soup where two stalks are all I need.

It's easy to keep cilantro fresh. Do the old parsley trick and immerse their stems in a jar of water in the fridge. They will last for weeks.

But do try some. Billions of folks adore it. That should be enough recommendation for you to give it a shot.

BOILING POINT, JUNE 6, 2001 • Every now and then, a flavor trend surfaces, and in Jim Hillibish's day, he treated each new taste a culinary mystery. This new flavor—the foods were Mexican, for the most part—he traced to cilantro.

Mexican Bean & Cilantro Salad

(Serve with grilled meats or fish or add to tortilla stuffed with chicken)

4 CUPS COOKED BEANS, PINTO OR KIDNEY

1 MEDIUM TOMATO, CUBED

3 SCALLIONS, THINLY SLICED

1/4 CUP RED ONION, FINELY CHOPPED

2 TABLESPOONS FRESH CILANTRO, MINCED

6 TABLESPOONS OLIVE OIL

3 TABLESPOONS RED WINE VINEGAR

Tabasco or other hot pepper sauce to taste

Mix all ingredients, adding the hot sauce and salt to taste. Marinate at least 1 hour before serving. May be made a day ahead and refrigerated. Serves 4 to 6.

Salsa-Mexican Red

(Great for chip dipping, huevos rancheros, tacos, etc.)

2 CUPS FRESH TOMATOES, DICED

1/4 CUP ONION, CHOPPED

1 1/2 TEASPOONS GARLIC, MINCED

1 TABLESPOON JALAPEÑO PEPPER, CHOPPED

1/8 TEASPOON SALT

1/4 TEASPOON OREGANO, DRIED

1 TABLESPOON FRESH CILANTRO, CHOPPED

3/4 TEASPOON FRESH LIME JUICE

Mix the tomatoes and onion, blending well. Mix in other ingredients. Let stand 1 hour before serving for the flavors to meld. May be served at room temperature or chilled.

Cold Lemon Chicken with 'Fragrant Green'

1 MEDIUM ONION, CHOPPED • 1 POUND CHICKEN BREAST, BONE-IN

5 TO 6 CELERY LEAVES • 4 TABLESPOONS FRESH LEMON JUICE

1 1/2 TABLESPOONS SOY SAUCE

4 TABLESPOONS CILANTRO LEAVES AND STEMS, FINELY CHOPPED • LEAF LETTUCE

Cover the onion, chicken breast and celery leaves with just enough water. Bring to a slow boil; cover and simmer over medium heat for 15 minutes or until done. Remove from the heat and allow the chicken to cool in the liquid. When it is cool, skin and bone the chicken and slice it.

Marinate the chicken slices with a mixture of lemon juice and soy sauce for 45 minutes.

On a serving dish, arrange the chicken slices on a bed of lettuce leaves and sprinkle with the chopped cilantro. Sprinkle fresh lemon juice over the chicken slices.

Ask your guests to roll the chicken in the lettuce leaves, egg-roll fashion. This makes 10 to 12 rolls.

All-American Desserts
COBBLERS AND CRISPS

DEEP IN THE HEART OF AMERICAN COOKERY, THERE RESIDES A SMALL BUT VOCAL ANTI-PIE MOVEMENT. THESE ARE FOLKS LIKE US, WHO CRINGE AT THE THOUGHT OF CRAFTING A PERFECT PIE CRUST.

It's not our fault. The competition is simply too obliterating. You know, church potlucks, Mrs. Baker's signature pies. Nobody can duplicate these. It's all in the hands, and if you don't have her hands, you're toast.

The pie pinnacle is the flaky crust, that fleeting wonder that escapes most of us. They cannot duplicate this with the technology-produced crusts at the grocery. It's light, it's airy, it melts in the mouth ... it's impossible.

The crust conundrum causes gardens full of uneaten berries. If we could make a decent pie, that would be no problem.

Plan B: It's crunch time.

Crunch? As in the candy bar, the Cleveland soccer team, the cereal captain? As in the abdominal exercise, the TV cartoon, the '90s rock group or the Great Credit Crunch of 2008?

Belay that. We're talking mouth feel here, crunchy style.

At its best, a crunch dessert will make you forget everything you remember about classic pies. It's rich, sweet, so-simple topping baked over the fresh fruits of your choice, crunchy, of course.

Preparation time: 15 minutes. Satisfaction rating: 5 stars. Difficulty: zero.

The pie lovers fight back: "A pie with no crust is like waiting for a bus that never comes."

Well, forget the pie comparisons. An American crunch holds its own in the beauty contest. As for the taste, no pie can duplicate that rush of crunchy goodness and gush of fresh berries underneath. Ever.

All-American Dessert Parade

COBBLER: Any crustless dessert baked with a sweet-dough topping. Also known as slump, grunt and pandowdy, depending on U.S. region.

CRUNCH: A crustless fruit dessert with cookie-like crumbles of topping.

CRUMBLE: Similar to a crunch, usually served with custard or ice cream. In England, it means crustless meat pies.

CRACKLE: Brownie or cookie topping that is soft on the inside and crunchy on the outside.

CRISP: Usually baked apples with crumbs of topping including nuts, oats, brown sugar, sugar and nutmeg. Apple-rhubarb is most famous option.

BROWN BETTY: Layers of apples or pears, breadcrumbs and brown sugar.

BOILING POINT, JUNE 14, 2011 • You decide late in a day to go to a potluck dinner or somebody's party, so you need a covered dish, and you pick a dessert. Jim Hillibish had a selection of the "crunch" kind—call them anti-pies—that tasted great and were ready to go in minutes.

Casserole Crunch

Power up your next casserole with this:

1/2 TEASPOON MINCED GARLIC • 2 TABLESPOONS BUTTER

1/4 CUP SOFT BREAD CRUMBS • 1 TABLESPOON MINCED PARSLEY

1 TABLESPOON PARMESAN CHEESE • DASH OF PAPRIKA

Melt butter with garlic. Off heat and toss with remaining ingredients. Cover top of a casserole with mixture, bake for 30 minutes or until a crunchy, golden brown.

Honey-Crunch Fruit Topping

1/4 TEASPOON CINNAMON

1/2 CUP HONEY

1 CUP BROWN SUGAR

3 TABLESPOONS BUTTER, DICED COLD

1/4 CUP FLOUR

1/2 CUP SALTED PEANUTS, LIGHTLY CHOPPED

Combine ingredients and drop over sweetened berries in ovenproof dish. Bake uncovered for 30 minutes at 350 degrees, or until fruit is bubbling. Serve over ice cream, pie, brownies or nearly any other dessert.

All-American Berry Crunch

2 PINTS RIPE BERRIES • 2 TEASPOONS LEMON JUICE

3 TABLESPOONS WHITE SUGAR

1 TABLESPOON ALL-PURPOSE FLOUR

1 CUP WHOLE-WHEAT FLOUR • 1/2 CUP ROLLED OATS

1/2 CUP BROWN SUGAR • 1 TEASPOON CINNAMON

4 TABLESPOONS BUTTER, COLD

1/2 CUP CHOPPED NUTS, OPTIONAL

Grease a 9-by-9-inch baking pan, glass preferred. Rinse berries in a colander. If using strawberries, cut off tops and slice into quarters. Pour berries into baking pan.

Dribble lemon juice onto berries, and mix. Add the sugar and all-purpose flour, and stir.

For the topping, combine whole-wheat flour, oats, brown sugar, nuts (optional) and cinnamon in a bowl. Add the butter cut into small pieces. Topping should resemble crumbs. Mix and sprinkle over berries in baking pan. Bake for 30 minutes at 350 degrees, or until berries are bubbling.

Serves 4 to 6.

NOTES: Whipped cream and vanilla ice cream are favorite toppings. Some of the most successful crunches are with mixed fruit, such as strawberries and rhubarb, blueberries and pineapple, apples and raisins or currants, peaches and any of the above.

THE WAY TO A WOMAN'S HEART IS THROUGH HER STOMACH

IN MY WIZENED OLD AGE, THE OCCASIONAL YOUNG MALE WILL TELL ME, "YOU KNOW, I JUST DON'T SEEM TO BE ABLE TO MEET GIRLS."

"Cook," I say.

"I mean, it's not like I'm a toad or anything, and I do have a nice SUV."

"Cook," I say.

"I have a pretty good place and a good job, and I'm not a crackhead or a drunk."

"Cook, cook, cook."

We keep hearing that ancient cliché, "The way to a man's heart is through his stomach." Well, the way to a woman's heart is through her mouth, en route to her stomach.

Learn from me. I was in the Army. My military haircut, amid all the cool guys who had hair down to their rear ends, earned me a subzero rating on the female pecking order. It got so bad, the pistol-toting WAC guard at the gate began looking good. The one rumored to have bullwhips in her bedroom.

Then I learned to cook, and the females rushed to make a reservation at Jim's Place. Amazing how they showed up at suppertime.

This is "cook" in the pots and pans sense, not the 1970s sense of "I cooked that chick."

There's something about a guy who can lay out a four courser plus a good wine and a baked Alaska that women find irresistible, and they tell their girlfriends. The potential of relinquishing a life of traditional female kitchen slaving is bonkers for long-term relationships.

If you don't think this is true, try a few artful meals on your No. 1. She'll put up with anything.

I attracted my wife-to-be not with romantic niceties or magnetic personality. At that time, I was driving an ancient Fiat 124 with a broken front spring and lived in a house filled with dirty laundry on all floors.

Our first date was a Boz Scaggs concert at Blossom Music Center. I packed the most breathless of picnics: chicken and asparagus in flour tortilla roll ups (before everybody was doing them), gazpacho salad on endive and a fine Italian white wine that cost more than the tickets. I threw in the ultimate dessert, baklava, from a now-defunct Greek bakery (sigh).

We had to take her Camaro Z as the Fiat 124 was broken down, again. The wonderful aroma from the cooler in the back seat kept the conversation lively and a relationship a realistic possibility.

After that came a steady stream of marvelous stuff from my little kitchen. She was calling ME, by the way.

We got married a couple of

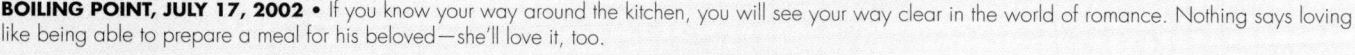

BOILING POINT, JULY 17, 2002 • If you know your way around the kitchen, you will see your way clear in the world of romance. Nothing says loving like being able to prepare a meal for his beloved—she'll love it, too.

Jim's Flour Tortilla Roll Ups

4 SOFT TORTILLAS, LARGE ONES • 2 CHICKEN BREASTS, BONELESS AND SKINNED

DASH GROUND CUMIN • DASH RED CHILI POWDER

1 PACKAGE CREAM CHEESE • 4 FRESH ASPARAGUS SPEARS

1 TEASPOON FRESH LEMON JUICE • 1/4 CUP FRESH CILANTRO, CHOPPED

Open the cream cheese and bring to room temperature. Boil the chicken breasts 20 minutes in water. Chop finely and season with salt, freshly ground pepper, cumin and chili powder.

Wash and microwave the asparagus for 20 seconds on high, covered. Uncover immediately and allow to cool. Dribble with lemon juice.

Mix the chicken and cilantro with the cream cheese. Spread on the tortillas. Place an asparagus spear in the center. Roll up and immediately wrap in aluminum foil. Chill. Pack in a cooler on ice.

Serves 2.

years and a near-zero investment in restaurant dates later.

That's how I became a keeper. I admit it freely, and have no illusions about the secret of our 24 years together. I've been cooking for her ever since.

She's put up with weird newspaper hours, computer-game and Web widowhood, love of entry-level cars and notion of Sunday romance (watching the Browns). We have a number of good friends whose marriages did not survive the same lifestyle. Just start preparing the meal at half-time.

As a public service, I'm providing our first-date picnic recipes. What you do after the picnic is your own business, but remember what your father told you, whatever that was.

Gazpacho Salad

1 MEDIUM TOMATO, CHOPPED

1/2 MEDIUM CUCUMBER, CHOPPED

1/2 MEDIUM GREEN PEPPER, SEEDED AND CHOPPED

1 CELERY STALK, FINELY CHOPPED

1/4 CUP SWEET ONION, CHOPPED

1 TABLESPOON FRESH PARSLEY, CHOPPED

2 SMALL HEADS OF BELGIAN ENDIVE

Herb Dressing

3 TABLESPOONS RED WINE VINEGAR

2 TABLESPOONS LEMON JUICE, FRESHLY SQUEEZED

1 TABLESPOON EXTRA VIRGIN OLIVE OIL, THE GOOD STUFF

1 TEASPOON DIJON-STYLE MUSTARD

1/2 TEASPOON OREGANO

1 CLOVE GARLIC, MINCED

Combine the first 6 ingredients in a flat dish. Combine ingredients for the herb dressing and mix until thoroughly blended.

Pour dressing over the vegetables, tossing gently.

Chill at least 2 hours.

Arrange endive leaves on serving plate at the picnic. Spoon salad on center of leaves. These can be eaten as finger food.

Serves 4.

HEEEERE'S JOHNNY!
(MARZETTI, THAT IS)

CALL IT JOHNNY MARZETTI, PERIOD. END OF STORY.

P.S. OK, maybe not. No recipe is more beloved, or bedeviled, than this stuff called Johnny Marzetti, aka noodles and ground beef. You know what I'm talking about, but you're probably not thinking about it the same way as I am.

That's because there are a zillion ways to cook J.M., and it has as many names. Just a few of them I've seen on local school cafeteria menus are Johnny, Johnny's Dinner, John's Dinner, Marzetti, Marzetti Noodles, and on and on.

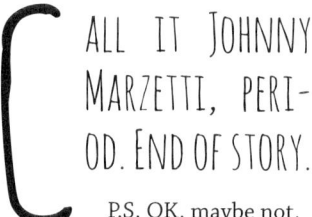

Even the Amish, bless their buggies, jumped in and call it Johnny Mazuma or Mazumma. Don't ask me why.

The only agreement is that Johnny M. is a casserole of ground beef or pork or both, noodles or elbow or bow tie macaroni, tomato sauce or tomato soup or tomato paste, and cheddar or Velveeta or Cheez Whiz. And, you cook it in the oven in a casserole dish or on the stovetop in a big skillet. Wait, did I say agreement?

Its beauty is it's always good and filling in all of its iterations, and it feeds a crowd. Leftovers last forever, almost, in the freezer, and make your microwave seem useful.

Many claim to possess the original recipe, but funny thing, all of these originals are different. There is some agreement that a guy named Johnny Marzetti invented the dish in his brother's restaurant in Columbus in the 1920s or so.

Some of you remember the Marzetti restaurant near Ohio State that closed in the 1970s, the home of Teresa Marzetti's slaw dressings. There's no mention of Johnny in that restaurant's lore, so who knows. Perhaps he was a black sheep who disparaged coleslaw.

Teresa's company later bought Inn Maid noodles, and on the package has appeared a recipe said by some to be the original Johnny Marzetti. Still, you won't see it identified as such. It's called Noodles Marzetti with Ground Beef. What a mystery.

Anyway, the following is a selection of Marzetti recipes claimed to be possible originals. Pick your favorite (I like the baked), and add your own magic. Then claim that IT is the original, of course. It tastes better that way.

BOILING POINT, JULY 11, 2001 • There are about as many different ways of making this dish as there are names for it: Marzetti, Johnny Marzetti, Johnny's Dinner, the list goes on. Jim liked his noodles with ground beef, and we have a suspicion the Johnny Marzetti he remembers most fondly first was eaten in a school cafeteria.

Baked Marzetti

3 CUPS UNCOOKED EGG NOODLES • 1/4 CUP MARGARINE

1 CUP FINE BREAD CRUMBS • 1 POUND GROUND BEEF

1/2 CUP CHOPPED ONION • 1/4 CUP CHOPPED GREEN PEPPER

1/2 TEASPOON GARLIC SALT • 1 TEASPOON SALT

1/8 TEASPOON PEPPER • 1 CUP GRATED JACK CHEESE

8-OUNCE CAN TOMATO SAUCE

4-OUNCE CAN MUSHROOM PIECES, DRAINED

Cook noodles, drain and set aside.

Melt butter in a skillet and add bread crumbs, browning them. Add and brown the meat. Add onions, green pepper, garlic salt, salt and pepper.

Layer the mixture and noodles in a greased casserole dish. Top with tomato sauce, mushrooms and the cheese. Heat in a 350-degree oven uncovered until cheese melts and the sauce is bubbly, about 20 minutes.

Serves 4.

Noodles Marzetti with Ground Beef

1 POUND GROUND BEEF OR SAUSAGE • 2 TABLESPOONS SHORTENING

1/2 CUP CHOPPED ONION • 1 GREEN PEPPER CUT IN STRIPS

1/4 TEASPOON GARLIC POWDER • 1 16-OUNCE CAN TOMATOES, DRAINED

1 BEEF BOUILLON CUBE • 2 TABLESPOONS WATER

1 TEASPOON SUGAR • 8-OUNCE PACKAGE NOODLES, EXTRA WIDE

1 CUP SHREDDED CHEDDAR CHEESE

Heat shortening in your biggest skillet, adding ground beef and onion. Cook until meat is browned and onion is translucent. Pour off fat and add remaining ingredients except for noodles and cheese.

In a bowl, mix a tablespoon of cornstarch with a little water. Add to mixture in skillet and stir.

Cook noodles and drain. Toss them with the cheese. Stir noodles into meat mixture, cover and heat until cheese melts and flavors blend.

Serves 4 to 6.

Johnny Marzetti

(SCHOOL CAFETERIA STYLE)

1 POUND GROUND CHUCK • 1 MEDIUM ONION, CHOPPED

1 GREEN PEPPER, CHOPPED • 1 TEASPOON SHORTENING OR OIL

29-OUNCE LARGE CAN TOMATOES • 29-OUNCE CAN TOMATO JUICE

1 POUND LARGE ELBOW MACARONI, COOKED

GARLIC SALT TO TASTE • SALT AND PEPPER TO TASTE

Heat oil and add meat, onion and pepper. Brown meat and drain off the fat. Add remaining ingredients. Simmer for 20 minutes and serve.

Serves 4 to 6.

INTRODUCING THE BEST POTATO SALAD
IN THE HISTORY OF THE WORLD

Don't you just hate it when you bring something new and have to take home 90 percent of it?

Once I made a nice (I thought so) creamed clam and herring dip. I'm still hearing about that disaster. The dogs wouldn't eat it.

So we have a year to recover our reputations. Be careful. Two strikes and you're out, permanently labeled a cook to shun forever.

I'm about to present you with a valuable gift.

This is not the best potato salad in town, in the country or in the world.

It's just the best you ever ate.

This one is from Pam McGowen. She's so well-known for this, she takes it to Thanksgiving. Everywhere she goes, "Hey, there goes Pam McGowen. Where's her potato salad?"

Potato salad has been around for a long time. Some claim it goes back to the 17th century. The Anglos mixed cooked spuds with vinegar. Soon, the Germans came up with their own version, bacon and vinegar salad served hot. That one survives.

The Italians combined their two favorite things, olive oil and herbs, in a marinated potato salad.

Pam's winner draws from a lot of that. She marinates her potatoes in Italian salad dressing. The main dressing is smashed yolks, mustard

and mayonnaise awakened with sour cream.

You can add any or all of the fresh veggies you wish. I like diced red and green peppers for color, chopped carrot for contrast and extra onion and chopped pepperoni if I'm playing dangerous.

Be sure to beautify it with sweet paprika. And don't just serve it in globs on a cardboard plate next to a burger. Make a nice green bed of lettuce to show off your salad on separate plates.

Remember: It could be the best thing on Earth, but nobody will eat it if it doesn't look great, too. Perhaps a sprig of parsley on each serving will help.

We must thank Pam for sharing this. I had to beg it from her after hearing the raves for months.

BOILING POINT, JULY 2, 2008 • It's especially pleasing in the world of food when you stumble upon a dish that is the best of something. In this case, Jim was given, and then he shared with his readers, "Pam McGowen's Best Potato Salad You Ever Ate"—the perfect food for summer picnics and backyard barbecues.

Pam McGowen's Best Potato Salad You Ever Ate

The Marinade

Use 1/4 cup of clear, Italian salad dressing such as Wishbone, or make your own with 1/8 cup extra virgin olive oil, 1/8 cup white wine vinegar and a dash each of salt, freshly ground black pepper and oregano. Shake to emulsify in a cruet.

The Salad

7 MEDIUM RED POTATOES (PONTIACS), BOILED IN THE JACKETS

3/4 CUP SLICED CELERY

1/3 CUP SLICED GREEN ONIONS, INCLUDING TOPS

4 HARD-BOILED EGGS

1 CUP MAYONNAISE

1/2 CUP SOUR CREAM

1 1/2 TEASPOONS PREPARED HORSERADISH MUSTARD (OR MIX 1/2 TEASPOON

HORSERADISH WITH 1 TEASPOON YELLOW MUSTARD)

Boil the potatoes in their skins; peel and cube to make 6 cups. Pour the dressing over the warm potatoes and gently stir. Chill covered, at least 2 hours. Add celery and onions. Chop and add the diced egg whites. Mash the yolks and mix with the mayonnaise, sour cream and horseradish mustard. Fold into potatoes with a spatula. Add salt and whole celery seed to taste. Add 1/3 cup diced cucumber, peeled and seeded, as an option. Chopped red pepper would be good, too. Allow the flavors to meld at least 2 hours in the fridge before serving. Pack in ice in a cooler if taking to a picnic. Garnish with paprika and fresh parsley. Makes 8 servings.

Double or triple for big picnics. Pam warns you'll never have enough.

IT'S TIME TO COBBLE A
blackberry heaven

"JIM, STAY OUT OF THE BLACK-BERRY PATCH." HOW DID SHE KNOW? OH, IT'S THE STAIN ON MY MOUTH. AND HANDS. AND T-SHIRT.

We anticipated the berry season with breathless expectation. Each year, the pesky bramble patch that tore at our skin (it was a magnet for baseballs) exploded with sweet blackberries. We picked them as fast as they ripened.

There's nothing like sweet berries still warm from the sun. Bite into that puppy, and it explodes juice.

The only reason any berries got home was my Mom's blackberry cobbler. This was a thing to behold, then to gobble. Even our beagle got involved, licking my plate.

Mom chose a cobbler instead of a pie. It's 85 percent less work on a hot afternoon. There's no laborious crust making that probably will turn out tough anyway.

Cobbler is as close to fresh berries as baking gets. Mom punctuated it with an incredibly yummy crumble topping, pure candy.

Her recipe is adaptable to any fresh berries or fruit. Just remember to serve with a glass of cold milk or a dab of vanilla ice cream.

My blackberry patch is groaning this year. Looks like an amazing harvest. I'll be rolling out Mom's recipe soonest.

BOILING POINT, JULY 28, 2010 • Cobbling together a dessert is a saying that has been used by more than one cook over the years. What Jim Hillibish cobbled together was a memory he called a "blackberry heaven," from berries he found in his own childhood backyard.

Blackberry Cobbler

1 TABLESPOON CORNSTARCH

1 TABLESPOON LEMON JUICE

1 CUP FLOUR

1/2 TEASPOON SALT

1 1/2 CUPS SUGAR

5 CUPS BLACKBERRIES, PICKED OVER AND WASHED

1 TEASPOON BAKING POWDER

6 TABLESPOONS BUTTER, COLD, CUT INTO PIECES

1/2 CUP PECANS, CHOPPED

Place cornstarch in a bowl. Slowly add 1/4 cup cold water and whisk to dissolve. Whisk in 1 cup sugar and lemon juice. Gently fold in whole blackberries.

Pour into a greased eight-inch cast-iron skillet or baking dish. Cook on stovetop for 15 minutes, stirring often.

In a bowl, combine the flour, remaining sugar, baking powder and salt. Blend in the butter until mixture resembles coarse meal. (A pastry cutter works well.)

Spread the nut topping over the berries. Bake 20 to 25 minutes at 400 degrees. The topping should be golden and the berries bubbling.

NOTE: Serve warm or slightly reheated in the microwave. Combinations of berries and peaches or pears are good. Go halves on each.

BEANIE-WEENIES NOT JUST FOR KIDS OR SOLDIERS

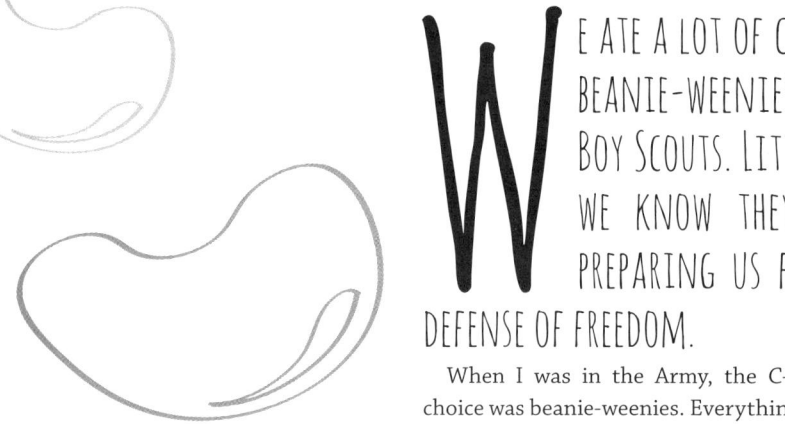

WE ATE A LOT OF CANNED BEANIE-WEENIES IN BOY SCOUTS. LITTLE DID WE KNOW THEY WERE PREPARING US FOR THE DEFENSE OF FREEDOM.

When I was in the Army, the C-ration of choice was beanie-weenies. Everything else, including congealed ham and soggy green beans, was deadlier than a land mine.

If you lucked out and found a can of beanie-weenies in your rations box, it was worth three packs of cigarettes or an equal number of chocolate bars.

Army guys become food crazies, making up for all the rotten meals they eat in the field. Beanie-weenies are one of the few dishes they prepare out of love and respect for the past.

My wife and I were enjoying bowls full when a friend stopped by.

"You're not eating that, are you?" he said.

"No, I'm just playing with it."

He could not figure out why anybody would eat beanie-weenies. Then again, he's not an Army vet.

There's a deluxe comfort restaurant in New York City that, alongside a grilled cheese, presents a nice pile of beanie-weenies for $20. So there, you food snobs.

The most common B-W recipe is a can of pork and beans and a pound of cut-up hot dogs. You must juice it up with a little brown sugar, Worcestershire sauce and vinegar, plus a dollop of Tabasco. Be sure to add chopped onion and peppers. That should get you through the night.

If I have time, I'd rather make the beans from scratch. Now this is a proper launching pad for your Sugardale Coneys. It takes a little effort, but the payoff is worth it.

So how did it get the name beanie-weenie? Nobody knows. I did have a college friend from Boston who called them "beaner-weiners."

In the South, they serve beanie-weenies on top of macaroni and cheese. Then they pass out in front of the TV. Too much comfort.

BOILING POINT, JULY 30, 2008 • It's summer and you need a quick and easy main dish that is filling and distracting—you don't want your family to wonder why there isn't a side dish in sight. A fall-back for Jim Hillibish was something he called "beanie-weenies," which, when bolstered by add-ins, satisfied both children and adults.

From-Scratch Beanie-Weenies

1 POUND DRY NAVY BEANS

1 14-OUNCE CAN CHOPPED OR WHOLE TOMATOES

1 TABLESPOON OLIVE OIL · 2 ONIONS, CHOPPED

2 GREEN PEPPERS, CHOPPED · 3 CLOVES GARLIC, CHOPPED

1 TABLESPOON WORCESTERSHIRE SAUCE

2 TABLESPOONS RED WINE VINEGAR

1/4 CUP BROWN SUGAR · 1 TABLESPOON MOLASSES

2 TABLESPOONS TOMATO PASTE · 1 14-OUNCE CAN BEEF BROTH

1 TABLESPOON BROWN MUSTARD · FRESHLY GROUND BLACK PEPPER

1 POUND HOT DOGS CUT INTO 1/2-INCH ROUNDS

Pick over the beans looking for stones. Soak for 8 hours covered with water. Drain and load into bean pot. Pour in beef broth and add water to cover. Bring to a boil and simmer until the beans are tender, stirring occasionally, about 2 hours. Drain.

Sauté the onions, garlic and peppers in the olive oil until tender. Add to beans. Mix remaining ingredients and add to beans.

Cook on low for at least 3 hours or until done. Add water or stock if beans are dry.

Add hot dogs in last hour. Serves 6 to 8.

Mom's Beanie-Weenies

1 POUND HOT DOGS, CUT INTO 1/2-INCH SLICES

1/2 CUP ONIONS DICED

1/2 CUP GREEN PEPPER, SLICED

1 28-OUNCE CAN BAKED BEANS

2/3 CUP KETCHUP

2 TABLESPOONS CIDER VINEGAR

1/4 CUP WORCESTERSHIRE SAUCE

1 1/2 TEASPOONS MINCED GARLIC

1 TABLESPOON BROWN MUSTARD

1 TABLESPOON BROWN SUGAR

Combine the hot dogs, baked beans and other ingredients. Bring to a boil. Turn heat to low, cover and simmer for 30 minutes, stirring occasionally. Serves 4.

Lemonade like Granny used to make

DEEP IN THE HEART OF THE GREAT DISMAL SWAMP ON THE VIRGINIA–NORTH CAROLINA LINE, YOU'D FIND GRANNY'S EATS, A STEAK-AND-EGGS JOINT WITH A PENCHANT FOR LEMONADE.

That drink was free to soldiers, so we packed the joint, not caring that Granny made it up fast with her chow. We had lemonade for breakfast, lunch and supper. Some guys would order a cup of coffee and get a lemonade on the side.

By the way, this was real lemonade, sweet and tangy all the way to your bladder and beyond.

Let's fast-forward 25 years. Lemons are two for $1, but I can buy a big bag of them for $4, so I do.

I'm lugging the bag into our house when I hear, "So now what's going on?" from my wife. I only hear this when I've made some grievous mistake, like putting my underwear on inside out or going to work on my day off.

Thinking fast, I blurt out, "lemonade," and like a 25-year locust, the flavor of Granny's suddenly crawls out of a quarter century of memories.

Nobody makes homemade lemonade anymore. It's just too darn convenient to open a can of chemical powder or one of those frozen concentrate tubes. Both, incidentally, are not bad, but real lemonade, from scratch, is eons better.

I didn't even have a recipe, but settled on this one:

BOILING POINT, AUG. 8, 2001 • Some in the South swear by sweet tea, but Granny—the one from Granny's Eats—wanted soldiers to drink her lemonade. The way Jim Hillibish recalled it, the cooling beverage also was the ingredient that helped her make the most out of Granny's BBQ Lemonade Chicken.

Granny's BBQ Lemonade Chicken

4 CHICKEN BREASTS · 1 TABLESPOON OLIVE OIL

12 OUNCES FRESH LEMONADE, REDUCED BY BOILING TO 6 OUNCES

2 TABLESPOONS BROWN SUGAR · 3 TABLESPOONS KETCHUP

1 TABLESPOON CIDER VINEGAR · 2 TABLESPOONS CORNSTARCH

2 TABLESPOONS WATER

Measure the lemonade into a sauce pan and boil until it reduces in half. Then stir in remaining ingredients except for cornstarch and water. Pour over chicken in a plastic bag and refrigerate for 4 hours.

Bake in the sauce 45 minutes at 350 degrees or until breasts are done, or remove chicken from sauce and grill over charcoal.

Mix cornstarch and water and pour into sauce, mixing until smooth over medium heat. Cook for 10 minutes. Pour over chicken and serve, or serve on the side.

Serves 4.

Lemonade Pie

1 9-INCH PIE SHELL BAKED, OR GRAHAM-CRACKER CRUST

6 OUNCES CREAM CHEESE, SOFTENED

1 CAN SWEETENED CONDENSED MILK (NOT EVAPORATED MILK)

1 CUP FRESH LEMONADE

1 PINT WHIPPING CREAM, WHIPPED

In a large bowl, beat cheese until fluffy. Gradually mix in condensed milk until smooth. Stir in lemonade. Fold in whipped cream. Pour into pie shell. Freeze or chill 4 to 5 hours or until firm. Allow to stand 10 minutes before serving.

Granny's (Actually Jim's) Lemonade

3 1/2 CUPS COLD SPRING WATER

3/4 CUP FRESHLY SQUEEZED LEMON JUICE, WITH PULP

1/2 CUP SUGAR OR TO TASTE

Mix everything and chill. If you like a really fresh taste, float lemon slices on top. Garnish with a sprig of fresh mint or lemon balm. For pink lemonade, puree 1/4 cup of strawberries in a blender and add.

Eats,

OFF IN THE WEST VIRGINIA HOLLER

MOST FOLKS GO TO WEST VIRGINIA TO HUNT, FISH, GAMBLE OR TO SPEED THROUGH TO FLORIDA. ON YOUR NEXT TRIP TO THE MOUNTAIN STATE, STOP AND DO LUNCH.

That means getting off the highway, way off. Almost every little town in a "holler" has a joint with a sign blinking "Eats."

If you cannot find one, stop at the gas station (I mean fillin' station) and ask the mechanic where he eats. He'll wipe his hands and climb into the back seat. Hope you have mud flaps.

Down here, the quality of the "eats" is related directly to the number of four-wheelers outside. Ambiance and portion control mean nothing. Oil cloths on the tables, 10-year-old calendars on the wall and no menus are the keys.

They'll know you're from Ohio before you hit the door, so don't try to fake it. Expect to hear the waitress say, "You know Jebbie Stewart? Went up to A-Hi-A in eighty-two."

"I worked with Bob Stewart in Canton, great guy, from down here someplace."

"Well, tell Bobbie to tell Jebbie Corine says hey."

"Let me get this down in my notebook."

You'll find a special scrawled on a slate board on the screen door. That's all you need to know.

"You wanna do it?" Corine says. She's already heard all the snappy comebacks to that. Just say, "Pray, let's do it."

Four minutes later, a pile of ribs arrives atop a mountain (not exaggerating) of cream taters (mashed potatoes) and hock beans (ham and butter beans) from the garden out back. And "cornbrad," all steamy and crumbly, with warm honey.

And swee' tea. Gotta have me that swee' tea.

This load is dinna, never called lunch. God knows what they eat for suppa, probably the rest of the pigsty.

You'll pay $3 or $4 for a special with free elderberry pie, or $2.25 to $3.25 without the free pie. It's an old joke, live with it already.

The food tastes great because it's so simple, and fresh. Homely homey. Maybe the best review is "real."

Those barbecued ribs you ordered? They're not smoke barbecued the Ohio way. Too much work. They're slow-baked in a stove oven. And just as good, even better. Fall off tenda.

The only thing dangerous

BOILING POINT, AUG. 7, 2002 • If we can generalize that all politics are local, we sure can say that all food is regional. Jim believed that one of the distinct flavors he found during his lifetime was the taste of food that hailed from the West Virginia "holler," and here are some examples.

Real Southern Sweet Tea

1 CUP WHITE SUGAR

1 GALLON SPRING WATER

10 TEA BAGS (WAL-MART GENERIC, NOTHING FANCY)

Place water, sugar and tea bags in pot. Boil for 10 minutes.

Remove from heat. Cover and steep for an hour. Remove bags and pour into a glass jug. Chill and serve in ice-filled plastic tumblers scarred by years of dish-washing.

about all this is you'll need a nap after dinna and three or four rest areas to get rid of the bottomless swee tea, which will last you to Carolina.

That is, if you get to Carolina. The mechanic will want to sit around a chaw a spell with the boys in the diner. Be patient, you'll never find the way back without him.

Anyway, Jebbie and Bobbie, if you're reading this, Corine says to say "hey" and "tell 'em about the free pie." That's a joke.

I stole this recipe from a woman named Murtha (not Martha), and not Murtha Stewart. It's totally 'cross the rivah, and you don't even need a Yankee six burner grill. However, you may need Corine's advice.

"You want a Pepto mint, six cent?"

"No."

"Here, on me, you'll need it."

Real West Virginia Pork Ribs

6 POUNDS PORK SPARERIBS • 1 TABLESPOON VEGETABLE OIL

4 MEDIUM SWEET ONIONS, CHOPPED • 2 CUPS WATER

2 BEEF BOUILLON CUBES • 3/4 CUP DARK BROWN SUGAR

1 CUP CATSUP (KETCHUP TO YANKEES) • 1/2 CUP CIDER VINEGAR

1 POUND CANNED TOMATO PUREE • 1 TEASPOON GARLIC SALT

1 TEASPOON CELERY SALT • 1 TABLESPOON CHILI POWDER

1/2 TEASPOON GROUND ALLSPICE • 1/2 TEASPOON GROUND GINGER

1/2 TEASPOON GROUND CLOVES • 1/2 TEASPOON DRY MUSTARD

3/4 CUP DRAINED SWEET PICKLE RELISH

Brown ribs in oil in heavy kettle. Mix remaining ingredients in a bowl and pour over ribs. Cover and simmer for 2 hours in a 325-degree oven, or until fall-off tender.

Serves 6.

COOKING UP A MOUNTAIN OF
ZUCCHINI

FRESH ZUCCHINI TASTES LIKE NOTHING, ZERO, ZILCH. THERE'S SOME ASSEMBLY REQUIRED TO UNLOCK ITS VEGETABLE POTENTIAL.

Zukers are in season right now. They're cheap in the store and growing by the thousands in our gardens. These critters grow so fast, so you'd better be out there picking the 4- to 6-inch ones or you'll have torpedoes by tomorrow.

Gardeners are willing to part with their crops, so ask around. "Got extra zucchini?" "How many hundred dozen do you need?"

Zucchini's great taste talent is it absorbs the flavors around it, quickly converting bland into a nice dish. The flavors can be as simple as your vinegar and oil salad dressing or as complex as a French wine sauce with tarragon.

My favorite recipe is baked, stuffed zucchini boats. Get some little Italian flags on toothpicks at your party store for a "garnish." You kids will love them. Just substitute zucchini for peppers in your stuffed peppers recipe, or use the one that follows.

Baking forces the flavor of the meat and sauce into the zucchini flesh. Each bite screams, "go ahead (insert your name here), eat another one."

Zukers are rather fragile vegetables. Always pick the small to medium ones, with waxy, tender skins. Some unscrupulous gardeners will try to foist the big guys with leathery skin onto you. They're best tossed immediately into the compost heap or peeled, seeded and grated for that great consumer of zucchini, the ubiquitous Z-bread.

For an almost instant side dish, heat a tablespoon of oil in a heavy skillet. Stem and slice three nice zukers into quarter-inch rounds, skin on.

Stir-fry in the oil for three minutes. Load into a flat, oiled baking dish. Season with salt and pepper and a sprinkling of dried basil. Spread a quarter cup of Italian white cheese on top and run under the broiler for two or three minutes. You could use provolone, mozzarella or asiago. This is great stuff beside a pile of pasta in a tomato sauce.

Incidentally, cubed zucchini is an excellent addition to your tomato sauce. Add with 15 minutes to go to keep its fresh texture.

BOILING POINT, AUG. 28, 2002 • So, you grew zucchini in your garden this year—and grew and grew and grew—and now the task at hand is getting rid of it all. Bish, the master gardener who liked to use all vegetables he couldn't share with friends and neighbors, had a few suggestions for the kitchen.

Baked Stuffed Zucchini

2 MEDIUM ZUCCHINI, 5 TO 6 INCHES LONG

1 POUND GROUND BEEF, Italian PORK SAUSAGE
OR LAMB OR A COMBINATION

1 SWEET ONION, DICED

1 CUP LONG-GRAIN RICE, COOKED

1 CLOVE GARLIC, MINCED

2 EGGS, LIGHTLY BEATEN

1/2 CUP ROMANO GRATED CHEESE

1 TEASPOON SALT

1/2 TEASPOON FRESHLY GROUND BLACK PEPPER

1/4 TEASPOON DRIED THYME OR OREGANO

4 PROVOLONE CHEESE SLICES

1 CUP TOMATO SAUCE SEASONED WITH GARLIC AND BASIL

Preheat oven to 350 degrees. Cut zucchini in half lengthwise and remove flesh with a spoon or melon baller, leaving sides 1/4-inch thick. Chop the pulp. In a bowl, mix onion, garlic, Romano cheese, meat, rice, eggs, salt, pepper, thyme and chopped zucchini.

Stuff each boat with the mixture. Place in greased baking dish. Pour 1/4 cup of tomato sauce on each boat and cover. Bake 40 minutes. Place a slice of mozzarella on each and bake, uncovered, 10 minutes.

Serve as a main course with a side of pasta tossed in olive oil, garlic and oregano. Don't forget the paper Italian flags on toothpicks.

Serves 4.

The Ubiquitous Z-Bread Recipe

2 LARGE EGGS • 1/2 CUP SALAD OIL

1 CUP DARK BROWN SUGAR • 1 1/2 CUPS GRATED ZUCCHINI

1 1/2 CUPS ALL PURPOSE FLOUR • 1/2 TEASPOON SALT

1 TEASPOON BAKING SODA • 1/2 TABLESPOON VANILLA

1 CUP CHOPPED NUTS (OPTIONAL)

Beat eggs until frothy. Add oil, sugar and zucchini. Stir in dry ingredients. Fold in vanilla and nuts. Pour into a 9-by-5-inch greased loaf pan. Bake at 350 for 1 hour. For muffins, pour into 8 greased muffin tips and bake at 425 for 18 to 23 minutes.

Serve with vanilla ice cream or fresh peaches. Serves 6 to 8.

A SEASON AFTER THE HARVEST

Crossing fruits to create a
sweet, seasonal sensation

IMAGINE A FRUIT ALMOST TOO SWEET. THAT'S A PLUOT, A SEASONAL BEAUTY NOW PLAYING AT OUR PRODUCE COUNTERS.

It is one of Floyd Zaiger's family of plum spinoffs. He hybridized a plum and an apricot, resulting in an excessively sweet fruit, double the plum sugar, heavy with juice.

Its original name was dinosaur egg, obviously faulty marketing. So Floyd switched it to pluot, a combination of plum and apricot. He first chose plap, but that sounded too much like a disease.

The lesser-knowns from his California company, Zaiger Genetics, are the nectaplum (nectarine-plum) and peacotum (peach-apricot-plum).

Pluot genes are plum-dominant, resulting in a fruit that roughly looks like one. The apricot contributes the high sugar, a certain tang and lighter skin.

Pluots ripen in July for consumption in fall. They grow exclusively in California and Washington state. They show good keeping qualities for the trip east. Dappled ones are the commercial standard.

They are not to be confused with Floyd's other plum combo, the plucot. In these, the primary genetic driver is the apricot.

If you see pluots in the store, buy a few. Stores often get only one shipment a season.

Pluots star as a recipe ingredient or for a stand-alone snacking fruit. You'll need a napkin, and don't wear your good clothes.

My family likes pluots in salads. They make wonderful jams and plum sauces for fish and poultry. Substitute them for plums in fruit pies and tarts, no extra sugar needed.

The food world keeps wondering what will be next from Mr. Zaiger. Well, he's working on combining a plum with a cherry. He calls it the cherum. Could have guessed that.

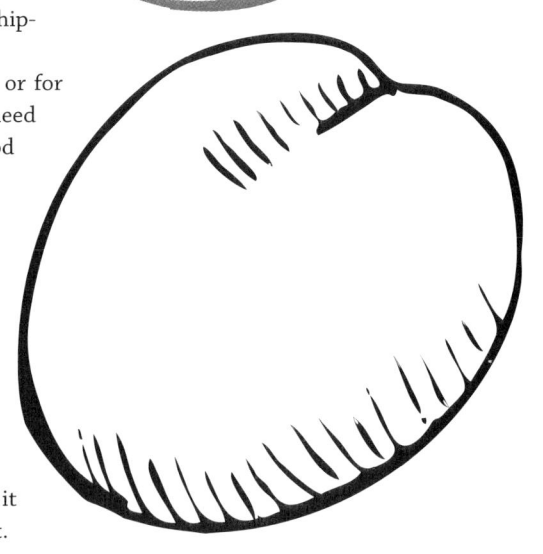

BOILING POINT, SEPT. 9, 2009 • An avid and knowledgeable gardener—Jim Hillibish penned Greenspace columns to share his wisdom—Bish always was in tune with seasonal treats. In one column, when pluots came to store shelves, Jim told his reader a little of the fruit's history and a special way in which to serve it: pluot salad.

Dressing

2 TABLESPOONS RICE VINEGAR

1 TABLESPOON LEMON JUICE

2 TABLESPOONS CHOPPED SHALLOT OR SCALLION

1/2 TEASPOON CHOPPED GRATED FRESH GINGER

1/4 TEASPOON HORSERADISH

1/2 TEASPOON POPPY SEEDS

1/3 CUP VEGETABLE OIL

Salad

3 CUPS LETTUCE GREENS

1/2 CUP CHOPPED SALTED ROASTED PEANUTS, DIVIDED

1 POUND PLUOTS, HALVED, PITTED, THINLY SLICED

1 POUND GRILLED CHICKEN BREAST, SLICED

1/4 CUP CHOPPED GREEN ONIONS

Blend dressing ingredients in a food processor until smooth, then chill for an hour. Toss lettuce with the dressing and half of the peanuts. Thinly slice chicken and place on top. Top with remaining peanuts and the dressing.

OPTIONAL: 1/2 cup peeled and thinly sliced jicama.

Serves 4.

CHILI TIME IS
CORNBREAD TIME

CHILI DEMANDS CORN-BREAD, THE SIDE DISH WITH A PURPOSE.

Cornbread is an excellent sop for spicy chili. Judges at chili championships use it to clear their palates.

Today's recipe adds two components not normally found in Southern-style cornbread: bacon and buttermilk. The bacon adds a smoky hint, while the buttermilk creates a tang not unlike sourdough, sans the bother.

Traditional cornbread always is made in a greased, cast-iron skillet, which imparts a slightly iron flavor. In the South, cornbread baked in iron is called pone. If you don't have an iron skillet, use a baking dish.

Sifting the dry ingredients creates a light and fluffy bread. Don't worry about little clumps of flour in the batter—over-mixing creates tougher bread.

BOILING POINT, SEPT. 23, 2010 • Is there a better match for cooling days than cornbread made to eat with warming of bowls of chili Jim Hillibish added bacon to his cornbread and told readers that it took the edge off of especially spicy chili.

Jim's Bacon Cornbread

3 STRIPS BACON

1 CUP YELLOW CORNMEAL

1 CUP FLOUR

4 TEASPOONS BAKING POWDER

1 TABLESPOON HONEY

1 CUP BUTTERMILK

1 LARGE EGG

3/4 TEASPOON SALT

1 CUP CHEDDAR CHEESE (OPTIONAL)

PAPRIKA

Fry the bacon in a cast-iron skillet, drain on paper towels and crumble. Lightly beat egg and honey into buttermilk. Sift together flour, cornmeal, baking powder and salt. Add bacon, milk and egg and lightly beat until batter just forms.

Pour into the iron skillet with 2 tablespoons of the bacon drippings. Bake at 400 degrees for 25 minutes. The bread is done when a toothpick inserted in the center comes out clean. Optional: Dust the top with paprika before baking. After baking, top with cheddar cheese and return to warm oven to melt.

Cut into 12 wedges. Serve with butter and apple butter.

Spice up your life with homemade salsa

KETCHUP NEVER IMPRESSED ME. OUR LITTLE BOTTLE JUST SITS THERE IN THE FRIDGE, LONELY.

But salsa—now you have something. It's ketchup at 95 mph. Although it has not yet made its way to our breakfast corn flakes, we seem to be eating it on everything else at my house.

A serious salsa habit will set you back serious bucks. Those little $3 jars add up fast. Homemade is the solution. It tastes much fresher, and you can make a couple of QUARTS for the price of one skimpy jar. Plus, it's so easy to make, anybody can do it in a few minutes. If you like salsa, you'll crave your own. Folks will demand you bring it to their parties.

Besides price, my main carp against commercial salsa is its salt. Like with most processed foods, they load it on, and it masks the true flavors of the condiment. Make your own, and you will power salsa to a new level.

The other problem, a typical one at our house, is pepper heat. I like it chunky and paint-stripping hot. My wife likes it smooth with just a hint of hot pepper. So we have his-and-hers jars, customized to our tastes.

Oh, one more problem. True salsa is uncooked. It's as fresh and bright as a tomato on the vine. The commercial version must be cooked, mushing its flavors. I like to taste each ingredient, so I like it fresh.

Here's your starter recipe, containing all of the essential ingredients.

BOILING POINT, OCT. 4, 2000 • Football games begin in the fall, and when there are games to watch, there also are mouths to feed. Jim Hillibish knew hosts could feed fans salsa out of a jar for their chips. But, homemade salsa made more culinary sense—and economical sense, as well.

Basic No-Heat Red Salsa

5 MEDIUM TOMATOES, CORED, PEELED AND SEEDED

1 TABLESPOON DICED GARLIC, LESS IF YOU PREFER

1 LARGE BELL PEPPER

1 MEDIUM SWEET ONION

1 TABLESPOON VINEGAR OR MORE TO YOUR TASTE

1 TEASPOON HONEY

1 DASH OF TABASCO OR OTHER PEPPER SAUCE

1/4 CUP FRESH CHOPPED PARSLEY OR CILANTRO (MORE AUTHENTIC)

This makes about 2 cups. Feel free to adjust the above to your own taste.

If you like chunky style, rough-chop the tomatoes and add the rest of the ingredients. If you like smooth, mix everything in a blender.

It's important to allow salsa to stand at least 3 hours in the refrigerator to develop the flavors.

I like heat, so I'd fire it up with 2 diced jalapeño peppers and a sprinkling of chipotle or chili powder. If you really want it hot, use 1 habañero pepper.

Fresh salsa must be refrigerated. It will last for a week. It freezes well, but only in the blender version. Frozen tomato chunks will lose their texture. You can cook and can it if you really want to go into production.

Salsa Verde is green salsa and made with tomatillos instead of tomatoes. These little green tomato-looking globes are hard to find in stores. I grow my own.

How to use salsa beyond a tortilla chip dipper is your choice. My salsa uses range from roast-beef sandwiches to a hot sauce on seafood. I've baked a Sunday pork or beef roast in it. It's a must cooked with enchiladas (sprinkle on some cumin); and it's perfect on tacos. You'll be amazed at how often you'll use it once you have an unlimited supply.

I enjoy experimenting with fusion cookery, where you combine various ethnic cuisines into something new. So, I like salsa half and half with Italian tomato sauce and Italian sausage baked with zita pasta with German Muenster cheese on top. Now that's fusion.

I was cooking scrambled eggs one morning when I thought, why not? I fried the eggs in a large skillet to get a quarter-inch thin, crepe-like result. Then I smeared on the salsa and jelly-rolled them, melting some cheddar cheese on top under the broiler. This is huevos rancheros, new style.

The corn flakes sat on the shelf that morning.

HOMEMADE APPLE BUTTER
goes with everything

APPLE BUTTER CAUSES TEARS OF NOSTALGIA IN YOUR EYES, ESPECIALLY IF YOU SPEND A COLD DAY OUTSIDE STIRRING A HUGE KETTLE OF IT OVER A WOOD FIRE.

Smuckers and the others do a pretty good job on this noble condiment, but homemade, with its smoky tang, is worth the bother, especially if you're selling it at $6 a jar to tourists.

Too bad fresh apple butter rarely gets beyond its Oktoberfest reputation. Certainly, warm muffins are a good landing spot for it, but you can use good old apple butter to power some recipes, too.

My great-grandfather loved apple butter atop cottage cheese. We just sat there watching him eat it, our eyes wide. He told us it was German. Now we know why they lost the wars.

I like apple butter on peanut butter and on buttered bread. There's no room for any more butter. If I make this for my work lunch, not only will the lunch room stare, the apple butter will sog the bread. So I bake the apple butter INTO the bread. Believe me, it works, and makes some fine toast.

You can create a faithful apple butter on the stove, but be ready to stir for hours. Your body will be perfumed with the sweet aroma for days, and you'll need some Tylenol for your muscles.

A modern way to make a good

BOILING POINT, OCT. 31, 2001 • Autumn is the season for apple butter, and the image of paddle-wielding churners mixing kettles of the stuff often is used to promote fall festivals. But, apple butter also can be made at home, at much lower a cost than buying jars of it, and there are many uses for the sweet and sticky stuff, such as bread.

Apple Butter Bread

1 1/2 TEASPOONS YEAST

1 CUP WHOLE WHEAT FLOUR

2 CUPS WHITE BREAD OR ALL-PURPOSE FLOUR

1 TEASPOON SALT

1 TABLESPOON SUGAR

3/4 CUP APPLE BUTTER

2 TABLESPOONS VEGETABLE OIL

3/4 CUP WATER

Dump ingredients into your machine in the order specified by the manufacturer. Set controls to large loaf, regular crust and start the machine.

To make by hand, add yeast to the flours, salt and sugar. Stir in the oil first, then the water and then the apple butter.

Mix until the dough is satiny, then knead by hand for 10 minutes.

Add more flour if dough is too sticky or a little water if it is too dry. Place in a greased bowl in a warm place, covered, to rise for an hour.

Punch down dough and knead for 10 minutes. Form into a ball. Dust a round baking brick or pizza pan with cornmeal and place the ball in the center. Cover and allow to rise in a warm place for another hour.

Brush milk on top of the loaf. Bake in a 350-degree oven for 30 minutes or until a toothpick comes out clean.

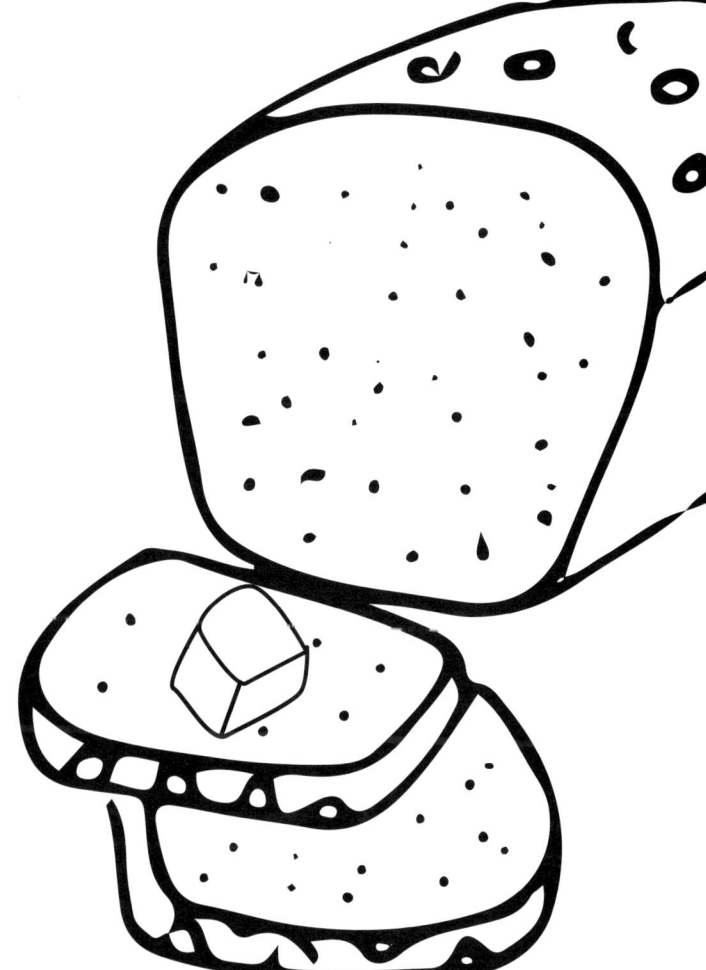

apple butter is in your crockpot. Simply peel, core and slice 4 pounds of sweet apples. Stuff as many as you can into your pot. Cover and heat on high for 2 hours. Then reduce to low and allow the apples to cook overnight.

Next morning, stir in 2 teaspoons ground cinnamon and 1/2 teaspoon of ground cloves or to taste. If you want a smooth apple butter, run it through your blender in small batches. This freezes well.

If that seems a little much, and all you have is a jar of applesauce, you have the makings of a quick apple butter. Try this:

Mix 1 1/2 teaspoons of ground cinnamon and 1/2 teaspoon each of ground cloves and ground allspice with 32 ounces of applesauce. Heat on low, uncovered, for an hour, stirring occasionally to thicken and, voila, almost instant apple butter for your toast, waffles or whatever.

Apples go well with cheese, so why not apple butter? Soften 4 ounces of cream cheese to room temperature. Place it in your food processor with 1/4 teaspoon vanilla extract and a dash of ground cinnamon. Process until well blended. This is fairly marvelous on crackers as a late-night or after-school snack.

If you have a breadmaker, the recipe is a cinch. Otherswise crank up your muscle.

How to make sorbet at home

YOU MIGHT BE TEMPTED TO WRITE OFF SORBET AS A CASUALTY OF OUR TERRIBLY SKEWERED ECONOMY. ITS PRICE INCREASES HAVE BEEN BRUTAL, OFTEN TAKING 25-CENT LEAPS.

Well, forget that. Make your own for way less than $2 for six servings. Exchange about 15 minutes of labor (not counting freezing) for a fresh batch that is sure to blow away your guests.

Sorbet is not just for dessert. Italians eat/slurp sorbet to prep palates before the main course. It works.

The optional alcohol in the adult version lowers its freezing temperature, resulting in a softer texture that screams "more." Don't be tempted to run it through a blender. Sorbet is not a smoothie. It is dense and packed with natural fruit flavor.

There are a lot of items similar to sorbet but not the real thing. Don't call it "sherbet." That's made with milk or cream. There never are egg or milk products in true sorbet.

A Slurpee is made from freezing soda pop. A snow cone is shaved ice with fruit-flavored sugar syrup, often artificial, dumped on top. Neither approach the startling flavor of sorbet.

The key to good sorbet is fresh fruit juice. This orange recipe is my favorite, garnering a blast of flavor from the oil in fresh orange peels. I'd serve it with chilled orange slices to complete the rapture.

BOILING POINT, OCT. 10, 2012 • A sorbet is the sophisticated frozen fruit drink—made from real fruit instead of fruit soda. As it rose quickly in price a few years ago, Jim Hillibish's interest in re-creating it at home also increased, until he offered a recipe for creating it to readers.

Really Orange Sorbet

1 CUP WATER

1/2 CUP SUGAR

PEEL OF 1 ORANGE, JULIENNED, WITHOUT WHITE PITH

2 CUPS FRESH ORANGE JUICE, THE REAL STUFF

2 TABLESPOONS ORANGE JUICE FROZEN CONCENTRATE

1 TABLESPOON GRAND MARNIER ORANGE LIQUEUR, OPTIONAL

Combine water, sugar and orange peel, bring to a boil, lower to medium and simmer 5 minutes. Cool and discard orange peel.

Combine syrup, orange juice, orange concentrate and Grand Marnier. If you have an ice-cream maker, freeze for 20 minutes. Or place in a bowl and freeze. When ice forms around the edges, stir with spatula. Continue the freeze-stir routine until sorbet has proper texture, about three times. Hard freeze if not used immediately, then defrost somewhat just before serving.

Garnish with chilled, fresh-orange slices. Serves 6.

USING HIS NOODLE—
IT'S EASY & FUN

I COULD TELL BY THE WAY THE PHONE RANG. THIS WAS A 911 CALL.

"I'm almost done with this recipe, but I'm out of noodles."

He answered my knock, and I handed him a ball of wet dough.

"Noodles," I said.

I know, some of you are cringing at the thought of homemade noodles. You have those visions of your grandmother slaving over cauldrons of boiling water, rolling out and cutting noodles by the thousands all day until her arthritis sent her to bed.

I've found some old noodles for new nerds. These take only minutes to make, are impossible to ruin and don't require any fancy hardware from Bologna or Dusseldorf, or a great grandmother, for that matter.

We make spaetzles (rhymes with pretzels) at my house when we want a hearty German Sunday dinner staple that once graced many a table in our town. They save the day when time and your pantry are short. And you can make enough for a crowd during halftime.

Your main spaetzle tools are your thumb and forefinger. That's it.

The "noodles," made from common pasta dough, are more like miniature dumplings. They taste amazingly good and will surprise your family, They're so rare these days you'll only find them in fine restaurants offering expensive German cuisine.

If fingers are too low-tech for you, you can cut spaetzles with one of those metal shredders your mom uses to make coleslaw. Use the one with the medium holes.

The beauty of spaetzles is they're totally inert by themselves, but just try adding a sauce or gravy. These noodle wads assume the flavor of anything they touch and, indeed, improve upon it. They go from zero to 100 mph in the flick of a spatula.

Here's how to get started:

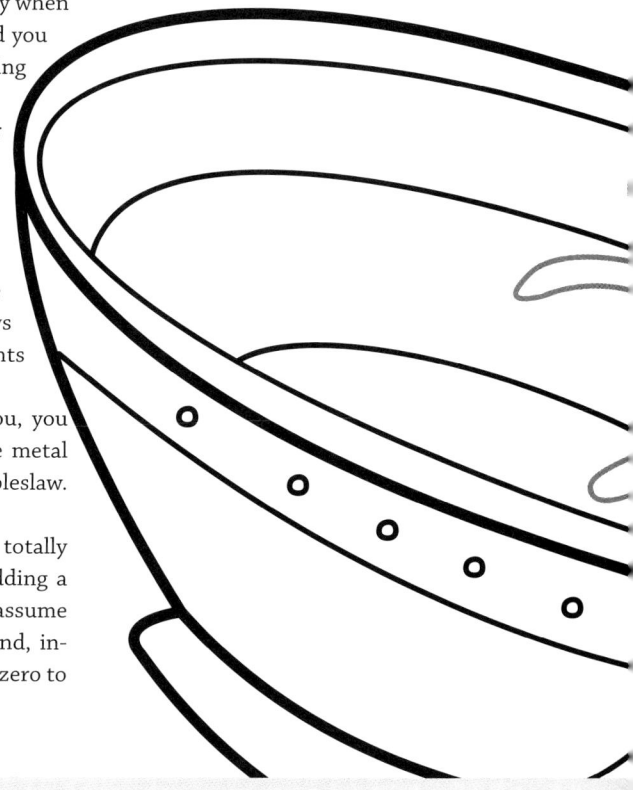

BOILING POINT, NOV. 29, 2000 • When it came to German spaetzles, Jim Hillibish was good at using his noodle. And the ones he produced took only minutes to make.

Sauerbraten Spaetzles

You can take your spaetzles into the stratosphere with Patti Unger's German beef recipe. The meat is very tender, and you won't miss the mashed potatoes:

3 POUNDS BEEF ROUND • 1/2 CUP VINEGAR

1 CUP WATER • 1 MEDIUM ONION, THINLY SLICED

2 BAY LEAVES • 3 WHOLE CLOVES • 2 TEASPOONS SALT

DASH OF PEPPER • 4 TABLESPOONS FAT

Trim fat from meat and reserve. Place meat in a glass or other nonmetallic bowl. Combine vinegar, water, onion, bay leaves, cloves, salt and pepper. Pour over meat. Cover and refrigerate 18 to 24 hours, turning a few times.

Melt the fat in heavy frying pan or Dutch oven. Drain meat, reserving marinade. Dust meat with flour and brown thoroughly on both sides.

Add 1 cup water to marinade and pour over meat. Cover, simmer over low heat 3 hours or until meat is tender. Remove meat, strain pan juices and stir in 1/2 pint sour cream. Pour over spaetzles. Garnish with freshly chopped parsley. Serves 4.

German Spaetzles

2 EGGS

1 CUP FLOUR

1 TEASPOON SALT

DASH NUTMEG (PREFERABLY FRESHLY GRATED)

Stir the ingredients, adding a little water to make a sticky but workable dough. Pinch off fingertip-size amounts into boiling, salted water or stock. Cook over a slow boil for 20 minutes or until tender. Drain, rinse and keep warm for serving. Serves 4.

Now you have spaetzles, ready for anything you'd serve with pasta or noodles.

One of my favorites is to simply brown the cooked noodles in butter and a little brown sugar. Served beside a thick pork chop and sauerkraut, this is not to be missed.

Another way is to fry the cooked noodles quickly in olive oil and dust with Parmesan cheese and paprika. This makes a good side dish to seafood when you're weary of rice or potatoes.

I adore spaetzles in soups, especially the venerable chicken noodle. They turn soup into hearty, stew fare, where one bowl is a meal and two a pig-out.

The beauty of these morsels is that unlike pasta, they're almost impossible to overcook. You can boil them ahead and reheat just before serving. I don't know anyone who has frozen them because they always are eaten right now and without leftovers. Besides, it only takes a few minutes to make a fresh batch.

The spaetzle secret is to be sure to rinse and drain them before serving. That's about it. They hold well in the cooking water, and it's easy to tell when they're done. The steam will smell like noodles, and they will float.

WHAT? GREEN BEAN CASSEROLE & NOT A CAN IN SIGHT

I DECIDED ENOUGH IS ENOUGH—NO MORE MUSHROOM SOUP GREEN BEANS ON THANKSGIVING.

This has been a family tradition for my entire life, a once-a-year treat, not.

We always traded houses on T-Day, but it made no difference who cooked the meal.

The souped-up beans always were, well, can-like.

My first Thanksgiving in the Army was at the home of my boss. There it was. Green beans mush.

I guess you can run but cannot hide.

I made some smart crack that, for sure, this was on my family's table. The others were surprised we ate such fine stuff up North. Virginians proudly claim it as their own.

I was a guest so had to take a glop. I tasted it, and my buds went up like an infield fly. Hey, this tastes like seconds.

It was Aunt Willa's recipe. She shunned the ease of canned green beans, canned mushroom soup and canned onion rings. Hers was all scratch; OK, not the onion rings.

She said make it a day ahead as it took time, but that was fine. The flavors melded.

The crunch of real green beans punctuated the soft caress of the creamy white sauce studded with mushrooms. Beautiful.

For me, it was an instant conversion. Instead of the usual hiding my beans under a dinner roll, I tore into them and asked for more. You had to move fast as the dish was the most popular on the table this side of the turkey and dressing.

I know. The canned version is so simple, your brother-in-law could make it, maybe.

It's a 10-minute chore, or less, usually after the turkey goes in.

Campbell's this season has a

prime-time commercial celebrating its legendary position on every T-Day table. This year they're shilling their Golden Mushroom Soup, calling it the Classic Green Bean Casserole, as opposed to last year's Legendary Green Bean Casserole. They say prep time is 10 minutes (you could do it in five with an electric can opener).

While making it fresh, you may long for the can-opener version, but kitchen convenience often is not the path to greatness. That's why day-ahead assembly is necessary. Then bake it beside your bird.

Try this. Don't say a word. Watch the faces. Better make a double recipe this time.

BOILING POINT, NOV. 17, 2009 • Whose family hasn't had an aunt among them who took it as her duty to supply the green bean casserole for family gatherings? Jim Hillibish's Aunt Willa took on the job in his family, and Bish fondly remembered the recipe.

Aunt Willa's Green Bean Casserole

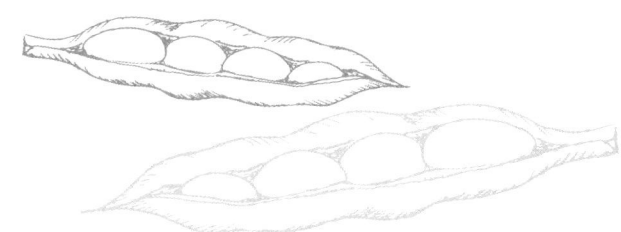

4 CUPS CUT, FRESH GREEN BEANS

2 CUBES BEEF BOUILLON

4 CUPS WATER

2 CUPS MILK

2 TABLESPOONS BUTTER

1 TABLESPOON FLOUR

1 CUP FRESH MUSHROOMS, SLICED

1 SMALL ONION, DICED

2 TABLESPOONS DRY SHERRY (OPTIONAL) OR 1 TEASPOON CIDER VINEGAR

1/2 TEASPOON TARRAGON DRIED HERB OR DRIED DILL

Clean and string the beans and cut into 2-inch lengths. Boil in bouillon and water for 8 minutes, drain, reserving 1/4 cup liquid.

Melt butter in a sauce pot. Add mushrooms and onion and flip around. Simmer about 5 minutes, then add reserved bean liquid and simmer another 5 minutes.

Stir in flour, making a paste. Whisk in part of milk to make a thin sauce. Keep whisking as it thickens, using as much milk as needed. Then add vinegar and tarragon and simmer on low 10 minutes, stirring often.

Place beans in a greased, flat casserole. Pour in mushroom sauce and stir to coat. Top with canned fried onion rings or potato chips or sticks, if that's your tradition.

Bake 45 minutes uncovered beside the turkey (350 degrees).

Serves 6 to 8 surprised diners.

Lucky or not, sauerkraut is good eating

December in Ohio is the month for sauerkraut. When those Arctic winds fly over Lake Erie to our doorsteps, we need the fortification of a good plate of steaming kraut.

The world treats sauerkraut in different ways. In some places, such as Poland, it's a pierogi (dumpling) filling. In Canada, they bury hot dogs in it. In Germany, it's served with great chunks of roast pork or ham—we're talking whole hog in some places.

Our tradition comes from Pennsylvania Dutch. They produced so much sauerkraut they had to invent a legend behind it. Hence the notion that eating kraut is lucky.

Holiday tradition

It becomes a fetish on New Year's Eve. The first food of the new year must be sauerkraut or you might as well stay in bed for the rest of the year.

Sauerkraut's not good for breakfast, so that meant cooking it for a midnight meal.

We still have a number of New Year's parties that end in a kraut feast.

Restaurants sell tons of it that night. No one can explain it, but nobody wants to chance a rotten year because they did not eat pickled cabbage.

I grew up with standard kraut right out of the can. I loved it raw, but my mom always cooked it with pork roast. The shredded cabbage at the bottom of the Dutch oven absorbed the pork fat and was something we fought over.

We always had mashed potatoes streaming with butter. I somehow latched upon Czech style, piling kraut on my potatoes. Still do.

A little tinkering

We learned over the years that we could improve upon this noble pickled cabbage. A native German friend of mine served me a

BOILING POINT, NOV. 12, 2008 • When the winds of November bring the snows of December, we need strong foods, and what could be stronger than sauerkraut? Late autumn indeed is sauerkraut season, and if you add a bit of pork and a few apples, you have yourself a recipe for success.

Sauerkraut Balls

1/2 POUND HAM, GROUND OR DICED

1/2 POUND CORNED BEEF, GROUND OR DICED

OLIVE OIL • 1 CUP ONION, MINCED

1 CUP MILK • 1 CUP FLOUR

1 TEASPOON DRY MUSTARD

2 TABLESPOONS CHIVES OR PARSLEY, FINELY CHOPPED

1 POUND SAUERKRAUT, CHOPPED

1 CUP BREAD CRUMBS • 1 EGG, BEATEN

2 CUPS VEGETABLE OIL

Coat skillet with oil and cook meat and onion. Whisk milk into flour, mustard and a dash of salt and freshly ground black pepper. Add parsley or chives. Add mixture to meat over low heat and stir until it thickens. Be careful of scorching. Chop kraut and heat in separate pan. Drain and add to meat mixture, cooking for 10 minutes. Cool to room temperature. Measure 1/4-cup morsels and shape into balls. Dip into beaten egg and roll in bread crumbs. Fry in vegetable oil until brown. Makes about a dozen balls.

Pork & Sauerkraut With Apples

1 14 1/2-OUNCE CAN SAUERKRAUT

2 TO 3 POUND BONELESS PORK LOIN

1 STRIP OF BACON

1/2 CUP ONION, CHOPPED

1 APPLE, PEELED, CORED AND SLICED

Fry bacon in baking dish. Remove. Brown pork roast in the fat on all sides. Pour off fat and add sauerkraut, onions and apple. Cover and cook over low heat for 90 minutes or until pork is tender, adding water if necessary. Serves 4.

giant plate with—what's that?—apples. The sweetness of the fruit was a beautiful contrast to the sour kraut. So that's the way I make ours.

Another worthy additive is caraway seeds, a prime flavor of German rye bread. They offer yet another contrast, a nutty, spicy flavor amid the sour.

I learned that the longer you cook kraut, the milder the flavor. For a bright, crisp plate, just warm it right out of the can and serve immediately.

Sauerkraut balls are a favorite appetizer, but might not contain enough kraut to bring exceptional luck. So you must eat a lot of them, which isn't that hard.

Cooking on

I'VE TRIED TO AVOID MENTIONING THE WORD "GAS" HERE FOR OBVIOUS REASONS. STILL, OUR NEW-RATE GAS BILLS ARE ARRIVING (YIKES!), SO IT'S NOW IMPOSSIBLE TO IGNORE.

You can save energy in the kitchen with a few easy steps. Don't expect to save a ton of cash doing these. Your furnace uses more gas in a day than your stove does in weeks. It does make sense to pinch every penny.

There's a concept called "cooking on" that chefs understand but few household cooks do. This happens when you turn off the heat but keep food on the burner, common to most of us cooks.

Due to the heat in the pan, the food keeps cooking. If it's seafood or pasta or beef you want rare, this can overcook it. As we get accustomed to our ranges, we must anticipate this to prevent problems.

Cooking on with electric ranges is more severe than with gas ones because the burner slowly releases its heat. This is why nearly all restaurant chefs use gas. I had an electric range for years and fairly quickly learned to adjust for this and used it to save power. Then I got a gas one and had to relearn everything.

A good example is popping popcorn. Have you noticed that when you turn off the heat, it keeps popping? That's cooking on.

Microwave ovens cook on more than ranges. Microwaves cook by sending high-energy beams into food. This starts their molecules jumping around, and this action, sort of like friction, creates heat and cooks the goods. The molecules keep vibrating even after the wave stops, for up to a few minutes. Microwave recipes often warn of this and build a standing time into the cooking length.

You can use cooking on to great effect. A lot of folks have trouble with overcooked rice. My way is to bring the rice to a boil in double the amount of liquid as the rice. Then I cover it, cook it on heat for 5 minutes and then off heat and let it stand on the stove for 20 minutes. The cooking on effect cooks the rice perfectly, and it remains hot.

You can do the same with boiled potatoes, pasta, vegetables and eggs, adjusting the initial heating time. All I know is when I'm cooking with the gas off, I'm saving money and eliminating overcooking at the same time.

A well-insulated oven cooks perfectly well with the heat off. I wouldn't do it with breads or pastries, which require a blast of heat for the full time, But you can do it with stews and roasts. I usually turn mine off when I reach 80 percent of the cooking time and keep it in there for the rest, using the freebie energy.

Another way to save money requires another physics lesson. If you can increase

BOILING POINT, DEC. 6, 2000 • "Cooking on" was a term that Jim Hillibish used more than once in his Boiling Point columns. One that was published late in the year of 2000 was a good explanation of the technique and the benefits a cook could derive from it.

Scalloped potatoes & ham

2 POUNDS POTATOES, PEELED AND SLICED • 2 CUPS DICED, COOKED HAM

1/3 CUP CHOPPED SCALLIONS • 3 TABLESPOONS FLOUR

1/2 TEASPOON SALT • 1/4 TEASPOON FRESHLY GROUND BLACK PEPPER

1 TABLESPOON BUTTER OR MARGARINE • 3 CUPS MILK, WARMED IN THE MICROWAVE

Preheat oven to 400 degrees. Coat a 2-quart casserole with olive oil. Arrange a layer of potatoes in casserole, then sprinkle with a portion of the scallions, ham, flour, salt and pepper. Continue to layer until all are used.

Dot top with butter and pour the heated milk over all.

Bake covered 20 minutes, then reduce heat to 350 degrees and bake for 40 minutes. Turn off heat and remove the lid. Continue "cooking on" for another 20 minutes with the oven door closed, or until the potatoes are tender.

Serves six.

A variation on this is to spread some diced cheddar cheese on top just before you start "cooking on."

I sometimes get creative with this and add a cup of fresh green beans or broccoli. The leftovers are wonderful right out of the microwave.

the atmosphere in a pan, you can cook in less time. This is the concept of the pressure cooker. Water boils faster and steam has greater cooking ability under higher pressure.

This is why a can of water will boil up to 50 percent faster with the lid on and save you some energy.

Steaming is another way to cook faster, and in many cases, better, as it doesn't boil out the nutrients. You can steam any vegetable and most seafoods in a few minutes. For a few dollars, you can get a steaming basket that will fit one of your pans.

Planning ahead will save time and money. One-pan meals save energy, and it's nice having only one pan to clean up. I often cook pasta directly in the sauce.

One of my favorite one-pans is scalloped potatoes and ham. Try this one and enjoy some energy efficiency along with a treat.

Beef Stroganoff stretches a little meat

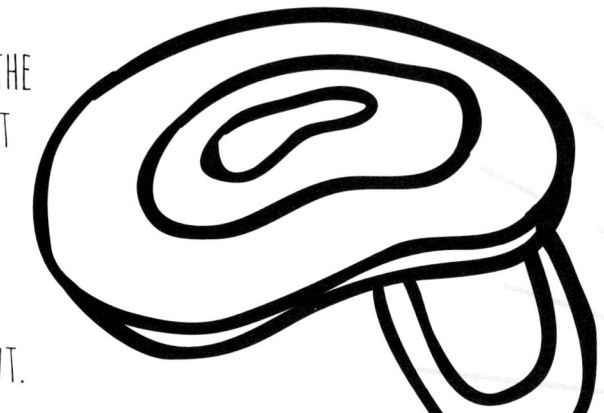

DEEP IN MY YOUTH, I REMEMBER THE DARK DAY WHEN BEEF SIRLOIN WENT OVER A DOLLAR A POUND. MY MOTHER THOUGHT IT WAS THE END OF THE WORLD, AND MY FATHER THOUGHT IT WAS THE END OF HIS BANK ACCOUNT.

Wish I could have invented a delicious recipe that was beef rich and fed four with but a pound of cheap beef. And I'm not talking ground beef.

Actually, the recipe was invented in the 1890s for a cookoff in St. Petersburg, Russia. It did all of the above, stretching a small amount of precious beef into dinner for four. Hence beef stroganoff, named for Count Stroganov who employed the wily chef who invented it.

This is a classic stretch-it recipe that makes full (as in stomach) use of a little beef. All together, it will make 4 pounds of food for four, with but a pound of meat.

Pound is part of the equation. Get out your meat mallet.

We all use sirloin tip steak, at $3.69 per pound. It's not filet, but is a can-do package for our beef desires. There's always some assembly required to turn it into a flavorful, tender repast.

Oh yes, the recipe. Its elegant name conjures the Russian czarist era. Tell your family you're having Beef Stroganoff and they'll wonder if they should dress up for dinner.

Stroganoff is tenderized beef cooked ahead in broth. It's finished in a gently heated sour cream sauce. Gently is important, as boiling will curdle it. Then serve it over plain noodles or rice and you have one tasty main course.

I've added two ingredients to the original recipe, a tablespoon of dry sherry and a teaspoon of celery seeds. They're optional, but not to be missed if you really want a showy meal. And don't skip the marinade and mallet. They're necessary to get that tough beef under control.

If you have leftovers (and you probably won't), throw them and the rice or noodles into a pot and add milk. This makes a hearty stroganoff soup, good with crusty rolls or biscuits. Unfortunately, the sour cream will not freeze very well.

Otherwise, do as the Russians do and stretch that pound of beef over four satisfying meals worthy of a czar.

BOILING POINT, DEC. 12, 2001 • What's a delicious recipe that stretches steak and feeds a family? Beef stroganoff. Jim supplied a history of the dish, along with a classic "stretch-it" recipe for feeding four with only a little cheap beef and a bunch of noodles.

Beef Stroganoff

1 POUND BEEF SIRLOIN TIP

2 TABLESPOONS SOY SAUCE

3 TABLESPOONS WORCESTERSHIRE SAUCE

1 ONION, LARGE, CHOPPED

1 SMALL CAN SLICED MUSHROOMS, DRAINED

1 TABLESPOON FLOUR (USE SECOND TABLESPOON IF NEEDED)

1/2 TO 1 TEASPOON CELERY SEEDS

1 TABLESPOON DRY SHERRY

10 OUNCES BEEF BROTH (CANNED OR FRESH)

1 PINT SOUR CREAM

Pound meat to 1/4 inch thick. Trim meat of fat and membrane, and slice across the grain into narrow strips. Then cut the strips into 2-inch lengths. This is easier if the beef is partially frozen.

Mix soy and Worcestershire sauces with a big dash of black pepper in a plastic food bag. Marinate beef in this for 2 hours in the refrigerator to tenderize it. Turn over the bag after an hour.

Cook onion in a tablespoon of butter in large skillet until transparent. Remove from pan. Brown meat in the same skillet and add marinade. Return onions to pan and add drained mushrooms and broth. Cover and simmer 30 to 45 minutes or until beef is very tender.

Stir in tablespoon of flour. Add paprika, celery seeds, sherry, salt and pepper to taste. Turn on low and mix in sour cream. Heat uncovered for 15 minutes, stirring often but do not allow to boil. If mixture seems too thick, add a little milk.

Serve over boiled rice or noodles. For 4, boil 10 to 12 ounces of noodles or 1 1/2 cups of rice.

Serves 4.

NOTE: For the English version, stir in 3 tablespoons of ketchup before the sour cream.

ELEGANT YET SIMPLE SOUPS FOR DINNER

THE SOUP THING REALLY JAZZES UP MULTI COURSE HOLIDAY DINNERS. BUT, FOR A LOT OF COOKS, IT'S THE ONLY TIME THEY ATTEMPT A HOMEMADE DINNER SOUP. MAYBE WE'RE MISSING SOMETHING.

Otherwise, soup is open a can or envelope for lunch. Don't even think about getting away with that for a formal dinner.

Soup as the first course of a major meal began in our world as an appetizer. Its mission: to perk up appetites but not smother them under something heavy. To this day, dinner soups remain light and fresh, happy food served in small bowls. Serve just enough and absolutely NO seconds, no matter how loud they yell for more.

Among Italian families, soup often comes last, with the salad. It becomes a light digestive after two hours groaning at mama's table. You always have room for a bowl, and your tummy will feel a lot better afterwards.

If you need a theme for an elegant dinner soup, remember simple. These are not your vegetable-barley-beef meals in a bowl, simmered all afternoon. They're ready quickly. This preserves a bright, fresh flavor, exactly what you're seeking in an appetizer.

Some chefs try to match their soup with their main course, even though the bowls are long gone before the big show begins. The idea is like wine selection, you know, whites for chicken and seafood, reds for beef and pork. This is more of a way to make up your mind than a rule of the table. I ignore all this and serve what I want.

My favorite "white" dinner soup is cucumber. It cooks in five minutes and has but two ingredients, plus a drop of sesame oil. For me, it's perfect. None of our guests has had it before, but a lot of them demand it when we invite them back.

Second up is cream of crab soup, an excellent starter for a seafood layout. You could spend a lot of money on fresh crab for it or use the canned claw meat for a lot less. Not many people will know the difference.

There's only one red dinner soup for me, and it's Spanish gazpacho. This one has only 12 ingredients. You serve it chilled, an unusual and delightful experience for many soup eaters.

All of these benefit from fresh-baked, warm rolls or bread. Place a roll on each plate yourself and whisk away the basket. Don't let anybody eat more than one. We're in the appetite-building business here.

BOILING POINT, NOV. 19, 2003 • It doesn't take a sophisticated kitchen to create an elegant soup, Jim Hillibish once noted. A cook can concoct simple soups that will "jazz up" formal meals at the holidays from some purely ordinary ingredients, such as cucumbers and other garden vegetables.

Cream of Crab Soup

1/2 CUP BUTTER • 3 TABLESPOONS FLOUR

1/4 TEASPOON CELERY SEED • 1 CUP CLEAR CHICKEN STOCK

1/4 CUP DICED SWEET ONION

1 PINT EACH OF MILK AND HALF AND HALF

1 POUND CRAB MEAT, FRESH, FROZEN OR CANNED

DASH WHITE PEPPER • SALT TO TASTE

CHOPPED FRESH PARSLEY FOR GARNISH

Melt butter in a large saucepan. Cook the onions until transparent. Whisk in flour and stir until butter is absorbed. Slowly add chicken stock, stirring until smooth. Add milk, half and half and seasonings. Stir until it thickens. Add the crab meat and heat about 5 minutes. Do not boil. Serves 6.

Gazpacho

2 1/2 CUPS TOMATO PUREE, CANNED IS FINE • 1/2 CUP CELERY WITH LEAVES

1/2 CUP CUCUMBER, PEELED AND SEEDED • 1/2 CUP GREEN PEPPER

1/3 CUP SWEET ONION • 2 TEASPOONS SNIPPED PARSLEY OR CILANTRO

1 OR 2 CLOVES GARLIC • 3 TABLESPOONS RED WINE VINEGAR

3 TABLESPOONS EXTRA VIRGIN OLIVE OIL • 1/2 TEASPOON SALT OR TO TASTE

1/4 TEASPOON FRESHLY GROUND PEPPER • 1/2 TEASPOON WORCESTERSHIRE SAUCE

Roughly chop the vegetables and place in a blender or food processor. Add remaining ingredients and blend until smooth. Refrigerate at least 4 hours.

Serve in chilled bowls. Serves 4.

Cucumber Soup

4 CUPS CLEAR CHICKEN STOCK • 1 MEDIUM CUCUMBER

SESAME OIL (OPTIONAL, AVAILABLE AT
ASIAN MARKETS OR GOURMET SECTIONS)

Peel the cucumber, slice lengthwise into quarters and remove seeds. Slice each length crosswise into 1/4-inch-wide "pennies." Heat the stock and add the cucumber. Simmer for 5 minutes.

Serve with a drip of sesame oil in each bowl. Serves 4.

SWEETS & TREATS & TRADITIONS

RECIPES ARE MOM'S LEGACY TO FAMILY

OUR MOM DIED IN APRIL. I SPENT MONTHS DREADING THE HOLIDAYS WITH HER EMPTY PLACE AT OUR DINING ROOM TABLE.

Mom believed God had a sense of humor. She always crafted a funny grace at our holiday feasts. Here's one:

"Dear Lord, bless these wonderful vittles, may they go to your glory and not to our middles. Let's eat."

Mom was no gourmet cook by any stretch. I rarely thought about her recipes until they were denied us. She insisted the family sit down together for all suppers, no matter what. There was no eat-on-the-go in her kitchen.

I have her recipe box, and everything in it is comfort food, just like her, always comfortable. If you don't have your mother's cherished recipes, I suggest you preserve them soon before it's too late.

My mom would not approve of our grieving for her, especially on Christmas. So we won't. We will remember her with stories and the holiday food she always served us from her recipe box.

It's not a bad thing to be remembered for your cooking. The food sparks recollections of family members and holidays past.

Mom always mixed her turkey dressing the night before. It wasn't Christmas Eve without the aroma of celery and onions wafting from the kitchen. Then she'd come out in her apron, and we'd sing carols and recite "The Night Before Christmas" in the living room lit by candles and the tree.

Truth be told, she always fretted the big meal, usually presenting it with, "Well, I hope this is OK." As if it wouldn't be.

Over the years, our holiday tables got smaller and smaller as we lost family, but the food never varied. I know the menu by heart. It's from her heart.

So we will gather once again on Christmas, secure our napkins in our laps as she insisted and replay one of her tricks. She tried to spark an argument about passing serving dishes to the left or the right, warning of a giant collision of turkey and fixins if custom was ignored.

We no longer dread the holidays without mom. We look forward to revisiting her as we pass her food to the right, cautioned by her "Jimmy, don't let your eyes be bigger than your stomach."

I'm including three of her holiday recipes here, written in her precise pencil printing on non-yellowed file cards. I never thought these would be important. Now I cherish them.

BOILING POINT, DEC. 21, 2005 • What was one of the greatest gifts that Jim Hillibish's mother could have left her family? Recipes—instructions for making all the traditional family meals—holiday and everyday dinners—that filled the stomach and warmed the heart.

Betty's Turkey Dressing

(FOR A 12-POUND BIRD)

2 1-POUND LOAVES WHITE BREAD • 1/4 CUP PARSLEY, CHOPPED

1 3/4 CUP CELERY WITH LEAVES, DICED • 1 3/4 CUP ONION, DICED

1 TEASPOON POULTRY SEASONING

5 EGGS • 1 CUP MILK

2 STICKS BUTTER • SALT AND PEPPER

Tear the bread into pieces in a large bowl. Melt butter in the milk and cool. Mix chopped vegetables, seasoning and eggs. Add milk and thoroughly mix. Refrigerate overnight. Stuff the turkey early the next morning and immediately begin roasting. Serves 6 to 8.

Betty's Baked Corn

2 TABLESPOONS BUTTER

2 TABLESPOONS FLOUR

2 TABLESPOONS SUGAR

DASH SALT

1 SMALL CAN EVAPORATED MILK
WITH WATER TO MAKE 1 CUP

1 CAN CREAM-STYLE CORN

1 EGG, LIGHTLY BEATEN

1/2 CUP FRESH BREAD CRUMBS, BUTTERED

Melt butter in saucepan. Whisk in flour, sugar and salt. Add evaporated milk and stir until thickened. Add corn and egg and turn into a buttered baking dish. Top with bread crumbs and bake 30 minutes at 350 degrees. Serves 6.

Betty's Carrot Salad

5 CUPS SLICED CARROTS

1 CAN TOMATO SOUP, CONDENSED

1/4 CUP OIL

1/3 CUP VINEGAR

1 MEDIUM PEPPER, DICED

1/2 CUP SUGAR

1/2 TEASPOON PREPARED MUSTARD

1 MEDIUM ONION, DICED

1/2 TEASPOON EACH SALT AND PEPPER

1 1/2 TEASPOONS WORCESTERSHIRE SAUCE

Cook, drain and cool the carrots. Combine with remaining ingredients and marinate at least 12 hours in the refrigerator. Serves 8 to 10.

From Hilda's Kitchen

HILDA MORHART'S KITCHEN WAS A CENTURY BEHIND THE TIMES WITH A SMALL STOVE IN THE CORNER, PAINTED-WOOD CABINETS AND NO ROOM FOR THE MODERN MICROWAVE OR DISHWASHER.

In this humble place, she cooked legendary German cuisine, stuff that helped shape her life.

I sat on a stool as she baked Kuchelchen by the hundreds. It was time for these marvelous, ginger cut cookies beloved for almost 100 years by German Separatists in Zoar. The small room filled with the aroma of spices tempered by heat and dough, a sure sign Christmas was near.

Hilda was the consummate German cook. One of the loves of her life was to preserve the recipes and history of Zoar, where her family, the Dischingers, settled and prospered.

Zoar was a Christian communal society begun in 1817 by 300 Germans who fled religious persecution in Württenberg. Everything was done for the common good. That meant eating together between hard labor in their Tuscarawas County fields, the workshops and the dormitories.

Children said grace, many times the simple "Father, bless this food for our strength and to your praise. Amen."

Let's eat!

Zoar was a closed society, and that meant its German traditions were unsullied by the outside until the modern world finally came in the 1890s. Then the society dissolved. Nowhere was Zoar life more apparent than the steaming tables of Old World food served three times a day.

This reputation for authentic German cuisine resulted in the Zoar Hotel with a large dining room serving the public. The hungry would come from as far as Cleveland and Columbus for foods cooked in the Old Country fashion.

Canton's William McKinley loved the place. So did travelers on the nearby Ohio and Erie Canal.

Hilda was the curator of this history. She still lived in Zoar. She was as prolific with a pen as she was in the kitchen. One suspects her favorite times were with a hungry audience in her kitchen repeating the story of Zoar.

"Now listen," she'd say, waving a wooden spoon.

She contacted relatives of the original settlers, assembling Zoar recipes. These comprise her small book "From Field to Table," which remains the bible for cooking German in Tuscarawas County.

Outsiders saw the Zoarites as plain, thrifty people. That translated to their food, although in this case, plain was also hearty and delicious. Everything was used. The water that braised the Sunday chicken became stock for Monday's Brown Flour Soup.

A large kettle of soup always simmered on the fire and changed character as the day's leftovers were added.

Potatoes were a staple, but they took them beyond usual with potato cakes, hot potato salad and croquettes fried in fat until golden.

The worst job in town was the baker's. He would start hours before every dawn, stoking his brick behive ovens with hickory. Then he would work his bread dough in large wooden bowls. There was no need to add yeast. There was plenty in the air of the shop.

The baker allotted so many loaves per

FEATURE, NOV. 12, 2008 • Jim's wife, Kathleen Fernandez Hillibish, once was the director of the historical site, Zoar Village, and he became well acquainted with its food tradition. Less than a decade ago, Bish collected for readers authentic Zoar recipes—foods from Hilda Morhart's kitchen.

Pickled Beet Eggs

1 15-OUNCE CAN PICKLED BEETS • 1 CUP VINEGAR • 1/4 CUP SUGAR

1 TEASPOON SALT • 4 WHOLE CLOVES • 2 STICKS CINNAMON

6 HARD-BOILED EGGS, PEELED

Drain beets. Measure juice and add water for 1 cup. Add remaining ingredients except eggs, and boil. Pour hot solution over beets. When cool, add eggs and let stand chilled in a large jar for at least 24 hours.

Hot Potato Salad

6 MEDIUM POTATOES, PEELED AND SLICED • 4 SLICES BACON, DICED

2 HARD-BOILED EGGS, CHOPPED • 1/4 CUP ONION, MINCED

1 EGG, BEATEN • 1/4 CUP CIDER VINEGAR

1 3/4 TEASPOONS SALT • 2 TEASPOONS SUGAR

Add chopped eggs to potatoes. Fry bacon and onion until brown and remove, reserving fat. Slowly add fat to beaten egg while stirring. Add bacon, onion, vinegar and salt, and pour over potatoes. Carefully reheat to prevent scorching and serve hot with salad greens.

Serves 4.

house depending on family size. Afternoons, he crafted buns, rolls and gingerbread for the hotel.

Zoar food often was served with religious meaning. The soft pretzels with a cross in the center always appeared on Good Friday. On Maundy Thursday, they ate something green, such as meadow lettuce (dandelion) with vinegar dressing.

Christmas meant spicy gin-ger cookies shaped into bells, stars and hearts.

Of course, there was sauerkraut, served with dumplings made from two cups of flour, a teaspoon of baking powder, a cup of milk and a beaten egg. Spoonfuls were baked in the kraut-smothering peppered spare ribs.

Hilda died in 1978. Her cookbook is still available on Amazon.com and possibly in used book stores.

Sauerbraten

The Zoarites celebrated fine, tender beef, and the long marinade of sauerbraten did the job.

1 CUP VINEGAR • 1/2 CUP WATER • 1 LARGE ONION, SLICED IN RINGS

1 TABLESPOON SUGAR • 1/2 TEASPOON FRESHLY GROUND PEPPER

1/2 TEASPOON WHOLE CLOVES • 2 BAY LEAVES • 3/4 TEASPOON DRIED MUSTARD

1 TEASPOON SALT • 2 POUNDS BONELESS BEEF RUMP ROAST

1 CUP SOUR CREAM • 1/4 CUP FLOUR

Mix ingredients and add meat. Cover and chill for 2 to 4 days, turning each day. Drain, reserving the liquid.

Dredge meat in flour, salt and pepper. Brown in oil on all sides. Strain marinade. Add 1/2 cup, cover and cook over low heat for 3 to 4 hours until tender. Check occasionally and add more if needed.

Remove meat, reserving 1/4 cup drippings. Combine sour cream with flour. Stir in remaining vinegar mix and cook until thickened as gravy (do not boil). Pour over mashed potatoes or boiled noodles.

Serves 4.

Zoar Christmas Cookies

1/2 CUP SHORTENING • 1 EGG • 1 CUP SUGAR • 1/2 TEASPOON SALT

1 TEASPOON CINNAMON • 1/2 TEASPOON GINGER • 2 TEASPOONS BAKING SODA

1 1/2 TEASPOONS BAKING POWDER • 1 CUP MOLASSES

1/2 TEASPOON VANILLA • 2 1/3 CUPS FLOUR

Combine and cream sugar, shortening, spices and baking soda and powder. Add egg, salt, vanilla, half of the flour and half of the molasses and beat well. Add remaining flour and molasses and beat until dough forms. Cover and chill dough for an hour. Roll on floured board to a quarter-inch thick and cut with cookie cutters. Bake on ungreased sheet at 350 degrees for 12 minutes or until cracks disappear from surface of cookies. Bake less time for moister cookies.

Yield: 2 dozen 2 1/2-inch cookies.

Pizzelles
UNUSUAL & IRRESISTIBLE

ONE OF THE GREAT ANTICIPATIONS OF CHRISTMAS WAS MARY COLETTI'S PIZZELLES.

Us neighborhood kids would start marching past her house on 35th Street NW soon after being let out of school for Christmas vacation. We kept hoping the front door would pop open and there would be Mary in her apron, beckoning us inside.

It always happened. Her husband, Pietro, set to regale us with Christmas stories from their homeland in Italy. And Mary, always the quiet one, would shuttle plates of still-warm pizzelles to our waiting mouths, and big glasses of cold milk to wash them down.

If we were good little girls and boys, we'd leave with paper bags full of the cookies, enough to last almost to Christmas.

We believed these Italian pressed wafers, with their strange shape and odd texture, were magical. We always saved the last one for Santa on Christmas Eve, in case he was Italian.

Mary and Pietro lived down the street from our house. They were our neighborhood's first-generation Italians and seemed like grandparents to all of us. We'd play baseball in the empty lot across the street, with Pietro our only spectator. We always knew when Mary was making meatballs, even a block away.

I'm sure the pizzelles brought tears to their eyes, a memory of the Italy they left behind for the good life in America. There was love in Mary's cookies, and we felt it.

Pizzelles are the oddballs of the pastry world, and perhaps that is why they are so deeply appreciated. All it takes is a few bites, and you are hooked.

On the cooking end, they're closer to a waffle. The iron press that creates them works exactly like a waffle iron.

Although you can buy electric pizzelle irons, the old fashioned ones, about $25, seem to do the best. You heat it over a stove burner, pour in a tablespoon of batter, close the press and bake 20 to 30 seconds on each side. The goal is a perfectly browned pizzelle.

I know, it sounds easy, but it does take practice. The main problem is to get the heating of the iron just right. Too much heat, and it will burn

BOILING POINT, DEC. 20, 2000 • The Boiling Point column in which Jim Hillibish revealed the recipe for Mary Coletti's pizzelles, published in The Canton Repository on Dec. 20, 2000, called the sweet treat "unusual and irresistible" in its headline. Jim's words unfolded a story that was part food column and much a memory.

Pizzelles

3 EGGS

3/4 CUP SUGAR

3/4 CUP BUTTER OR MARGARINE, SOFTENED

1 TEASPOON VANILLA EXTRACT

1/4 TEASPOON ANISE OIL

1 1/2 CUPS ALL-PURPOSE FLOUR

1 TEASPOON BAKING POWDER

VEGETABLE OIL

Beat eggs at medium speed with an electric mixer until foamy, gradually adding sugar. Continue beating until thick, then add butter, vanilla and anise oil (available in Italian groceries and natural foods stores), and mix well.

Add flour and baking powder, beating until smooth. Brush pizzelle iron lightly with olive oil and heat iron over medium burner about 2 minutes.

Place 1 tablespoon of batter in center of iron, close and cook 30 seconds on each side or until pizzelle is lightly browned. Repeat with remaining batter. Cool cookies on wire racks.

Makes 2 1/2 dozen.

the wafer. Too little, and you get a spongy mess.

You can only learn this from experience. Most recipes give only general heating times. A lot depends on your iron and stove.

Long-standing pizzelle bakers know by the smell of the iron when it's ready to press and cook and when that cookie's done. It will come to you, too, but expect to ruin a few in the process.

You want a cookie that is crisp and tender at the same time. The way to get this is to cool them on racks. If you stack them, they get soggy and gooey.

Mary would have pizzelles cooling all over her kitchen. She was a one-woman assembly line and could turn out dozens of perfect ones per hour.

Those of you unwilling to go through the work are lucky. Pizzelles are one of the few cookies that taste almost as good out of the box as they do right off the press. Many of the commercial varieties are excellent. Be sure to buy them fresh and keep them tightly sealed, as they get stale quickly in open air.

Here's the basic batter recipe.

A SOUP TO CONSUME YOUR LEFTOVER TURKEY

DO YOU HAVE LEFT-OVER TURKEY? WHO DOESN'T?

In my family, we always have soup on Thanksgiving night. It goes down easy after the carbo-holic main feast at noon.

Nancy Malone sent me a 9-1-1 email:

"I lost your turkey-mushroom recipe from a 1990 'Boiling Point' (column). Help. It's become our family tradition.

"I shortened it somewhat, passing on a 3-hour boiling of the carcass for turkey broth. Chicken broth works just as well. The creamy mushroom component is a disguise for those weary of yet another turkey meal."

BOILING POINT, NOV. 29, 2011 • If you have Thanksgiving dinner at your house, surely you will have leftovers. Jim Hillibish had a use for them—turkey mushroom soup—which he wrote about in a 1990 Boiling Point column, then, courtesy of a request from Nancy Malone, he reminded readers of it in 2011.

Turkey Mushroom Soup

6 TABLESPOONS BUTTER OR MARGARINE

6 TABLESPOONS ALL-PURPOSE FLOUR

4 CUPS TURKEY OR CHICKEN BROTH, CANNED OK

2 CUPS HALF AND HALF

1 TABLESPOON OLIVE OIL

1 LARGE ONION, CHOPPED

8 OUNCES FRESH MUSHROOMS, SLICED

3 CLOVES GARLIC, DICED

3 RIBS CELERY AND LEAVES, SLICED

5 MEDIUM CARROTS, PEELED, SLICED IN ROUNDS

1 TEASPOON SALT

1/4 TEASPOON WHITE PEPPER

1 TEASPOON DRIED FRENCH TARRAGON

4 CUPS COOKED TURKEY, CHOPPED

1/2 CUP FROZEN PEAS

Melt butter in a pot, whisk in flour. Simmer on low while in a soup kettle sautéing garlic, vegetables and mushrooms 6 minutes in oil. Save the peas for later.

Add to the broth mixture frozen peas, vegetables and seasonings. Slowly stir in half and half until slightly thickened, then add turkey and peas. Cover and simmer for 15 minutes, stirring occasionally (do not boil).

NOTES: Garnish soup with fresh, chopped parsley or spinach. Serve at the table in a tureen, or use as a sauce over warmed dressing, cooked noodles or rice. Serves 6 to 8.

PUNCH UP YOUR HOLIDAY PARTY WITH Champagne

IT'S CALLED A PUNCH BE-CAUSE IT HAS A KICK, ALCOHOLIC, THAT IS.

In the early 17th century, punch was king in India but almost nowhere else. A large punch bowl dominated dinner tables, ringed with glasses.

The drink was popular among hosts seeking a break from the usual cocktails. Another advantage: Punch feeds a crowd more cheaply than straight liquors.

After the custom spread to England, it rapidly caught fire throughout Europe, including Germany where "fire" became literal. Its Fire Punch Bowl is red wine and flaming rum poured over sugar.

BOILING POINT, NOV. 23, 2012 • Jim Hillibish often added tidbits of history to his cooking columns to give his writing a little kick. The alcohol in this party drink was what gave a kick to this recipe for champagne punch.

Champagne Punch

24 OUNCES FROZEN LEMONADE CONCENTRATE, UNDILUTED

24 OUNCES PINEAPPLE JUICE CONCENTRATE, UNDILUTED

6 CUPS SODA WATER

ICE CUBES OR ICE RING

25.4 OUNCE BOTTLE CHAMPAGNE, CHILLED

2 33.8 OUNCE BOTTLES OF GINGER ALE, CHILLED

28 OUNCES TONIC WATER, CHILLED

Combine first three ingredients, stir and chill. Just before serving, place ice ring in bowl and add remaining ingredients.

Makes 20 6-ounce cups.

DAY-AFTER CHRISTMAS TREATS CAN BE A REAL CHALLENGE

THE DAY AFTER CHRIST-MAS IS THE LITMUS TEST OF OUR CULINARY WITS. MANY OF US WILL HAVE OVERNIGHT GUESTS, PLUS EXTRA KIDS AND PERHAPS NEIGHBORS. FOOD STILL IS A FOCUS. THEY'LL BE STARVING BY BREAKFAST TIME, FOR SURE.

Despite all the holiday leftover recipes, folks simply cannot face another day of high-carbo, day-after turkey torture. But the last thing we want is to spend another harrowing 10 hours in the kitchen. We need good, fast and memorable.

We must come up with three easily expandable meals that, hopefully, folks will be talking about when they head home. This is the challenge of Christmas past.

For breakfast, a frittata is a must at my house. It's unusual, almost instant and a real eye opener. This is a Spanish egg dish that takes 15 minutes, and all will love it.

An elegant English rarebit is my 15-minute lunch. The kids will think you're making "rabbit," so the hardest part is allaying their fears.

For supper, I will roll out a pasta dish with a surprise meat ingredient that looks common but tastes like an Italian vacation.

Relax and have fun with these. Your guests will be so impressed, they'll offer to do the dishes. OK, probably not.

For the frittata, it's important to avoid overcooking the eggs. I like mine just cooked and tender.

BOILING POINT, DEC. 26, 2001 • The Christmas holiday is over, but the house guests still are hanging around your home, so you must feed them. In a Boiling Point column, Jim Hillibish served up solutions for breakfast, lunch and dinner entrées.

Breakfast Frittata

6 LARGE EGGS • 2 TABLESPOONS SOUR CREAM

DASH OF SALT • 1/2 TABLESPOON OLIVE OIL

1 POUND LINK SAUSAGE OF ANY TYPE, SLICED INTO ROUNDS

1 CLOVE GARLIC, DICED • 1 MEDIUM RED ONION, SLICED

1 CUP CANNED ARTICHOKE HEARTS, SLICED

1/2 CUP GREEN OR RED PEPPER OR BOTH, SLICED • PAPRIKA

Whisk the eggs lightly, mixing with the sour cream and a little salt. Heat the oil in a large, oven-proof skillet. Cast iron is perfect. Thoroughly cook the sausage and remove. Towel out the skillet, heat the olive oil and sauté the onions, mushrooms, artichokes and pepper, about 5 minutes. Add the eggs and sausage, gently stirring to distribute the ingredients. Cook on low heat until the eggs begin to set but are runny on top.

Run it under the broiler for less than 5 minutes, watching constantly. It's done when the eggs set on top. Sprinkle with paprika, slice in wedges and serve with warm buttered biscuits or English muffins and grapes, orange wedges or grapefruit halves. Serves 4.

Dinner Pancetta (Bacon) Pasta

1 POUND THINLY SLICED PANCETTA OR BACON, CUBED, RENDERED • 1 TABLESPOON OLIVE OIL

3 CLOVES GARLIC, SLICED • 1 MEDIUM ONION, SLICED • 1/2 TEASPOON RED PEPPER FLAKES

SALT AND PEPPER • SIMMERED TOMATO SAUCE

1 POUND PASTA (PENNE, GEMELLI, ROTINI OR SMALL RIGATONI) • GRATED ITALIAN CHEESE

Place the bacon into a pot of boiling water and render for 5 minutes. Drain and place on paper towels.

Combine pepper flakes, onion and garlic and sauté until translucent. Season with salt and pepper. Add bacon and tomato sauce, reduce heat and cook 10 to 15 minutes. While sauce simmers, boil pasta according to package directions until al dente.

Drain pasta and add to simmering sauce. Toss to coat. Serve immediately, topped with freshly grated cheese, such as parmesan or Romano.

Lunch Rarebit

3 TABLESPOONS BUTTER • 1/2 CUP WHITE WINE, DRY

3 CUPS OF MELTING CHEESE AS MONTEREY JACK, SMALL CUBED

2 CUPS FRESH MUSHROOMS, SLICED • 1 LARGE EGG, LIGHTLY BEATEN

1 TEASPOON WORCESTERSHIRE SAUCE

1/2 TEASPOON BASIL OR TARRAGON FLAKES • FRESH PARSLEY GARNISH

Melt a tablespoon of butter in the top of a double boiler. If you don't have a double boiler, place a small saucepan atop a larger one containing 2 inches of boiling water. Don't allow the water to touch the bottom of the saucepan. Add the wine and heat, then stir in 2 cups of the cheese. Heat until melted.

Add a little of the cheese mixture to the beaten eggs and then whisk the egg mixture back into the cheese. Cook and whisk constantly, about 1 minute. Add the remaining ingredients except the mushrooms and remaining butter and cheese. Set aside keeping the sauce warm.

Sauté the mushrooms in the remaining butter until just tender and sprinkle with the remaining cheese. Remove from the heat.

Arrange toast points or triangles on individual heatproof plates. Spoon the sauce over the toast and top with the mushrooms. Sprinkle with the remaining cheese and broil until bubbly.

Serve with a light green salad, rolls and glasses of white wine.

Serves 4.

Tomato Sauce

2 28-OUNCE CANS TOMATO PUREE • 2 TABLESPOONS EXTRA VIRGIN OLIVE OIL

1 MEDIUM SPANISH ONION, DICED • 4 CLOVES GARLIC, PEELED AND SLICED

1 TABLESPOON DRIED THYME FLAKES • 1 TABLESPOON DRIED OREGANO FLAKES

1 MEDIUM CARROT, SHREDDED • DASH TABASCO SAUCE

SALT AND FRESHLY GROUND PEPPER

Heat the olive oil in a saucepan. Sauté garlic, onion and herbs about 5 minutes. Add the carrot and cook 5 minutes or until the carrot is soft.

Add the puree, a few drops of Tabasco and salt and pepper to taste. Lower the heat and simmer uncovered for 15 minutes, stirring often.